My father and I

Journey of Alzheimer's

Omid Ferdowsi

For everyone who has
witnessed the pain of Alzheimer's.

Journey of
Alzheimer's

Introduction

On June 28, 2016, my dad sent me an article about one of the most successful college basketball coaches of all time, former Tennessee Lady Vols basketball coach, Pat Summit. The article was about her death as a result of Alzheimer's. My dad sent me a note along with the article that read in part "this is going to be me." I had no idea what was to come. He was 65 at the time.

Alzheimer's is a journey. There is no map for it. Nothing in life can prepare you for it. Those who haven't been on the journey have a hard time understanding it; some even disappear because the presence of the disease scares them. This book is for all of you who have been on the journey or who are going through it now. It is also for everyone who knows someone whose life has been touched by this disease. I hope to give you a glimpse of what life is like for your old friend and those who help take care of

them.

1
The Beginning

Shortly after my dad sent that text, I moved home for a few months while I was looking for my own place to live. During this time, I noticed that my dad would frequently forget where he put his wallet and keys. We speculated that he may have Alzheimer's because his dad had it and passed away from the disease before I was born. However, outside of forgetting where he placed things, he was still himself and still able to go to work for another year.

That all changed around August of 2017. Around this time, my father began to forget people's names and small details from the previous day, such as what he ate. This made him frustrated. We have all run around the house looking for our keys at some point. Now imagine doing that every day. Imagine looking for your keys and trying to retrace your steps when you can't remember what your steps were. The frustration of losing his keys mixed with the frustration of not remembering his steps would lead to anger outbursts that were foreign to his personality. Thankfully these outbursts subsided quickly but they showed up again a few years later (more on that later).

In September of 2017, my sister, mother, father and I all agreed that my dad should get tested for Alzheimers. Have you ever taken an exam in school, felt like you failed it and then just wanted to get the test back so you could accept the F and move forward with your life? That's how I felt about my dad being tested. I felt like having affirmation that he had Alzheimer's would allow us to acknowledge the issue and be able to understand how to fight it. Little did I know that nothing prepares you for Alzheimer's.

Not long after he was diagnosed with Alzheimer's, my dad started to care less about his job. First he left 10 minutes later than usual, then 15 minutes later and then he started leaving home around the time he had to be at work. Some of you might read this and think we were crazy for letting him continue to work after his diagnosis. It was a daily battle trying to get him to quit his job and not go to work. He was a grown man who knew something was wrong but did not fully accept it.

Imagine someone standing in your way and preventing you from going to your job or having people hide your keys. Should he have just given up on his life after his diagnosis and become dependent on others? How many of us would have been just as stubborn? Thankfully he still knew how to get to and from work. It was a habit that was etched into his long term memory.

Eventually though, he had to quit his job and that is when the first of many friends disappeared. He had a friend at work who he always spoke very highly of. You know how some people at work are just colleagues and others you stay in touch with even when you don't work together anymore? This was a lifelong friend. At least I thought.

After my dad was forced to quit his job because of

Alzheimer's, we never heard from this old friend again.

2
Where Are the Friends?

My father had friends dispersed throughout the country. He had a core of close friends from college that were in California, New York and everywhere in between. While he rarely saw these friends, he would still have long and in-depth phone conversations with many of them on a bi-weekly basis. He had a group of friends in Minnesota that he saw multiple times a week. They would go to the gym and play basketball throughout the week. On Sundays, they would all wake up early, go to the gym, play basketball games and then go out for coffee. My father was not one to wake up early but every Sunday he was up and out of the house by 8 am and would not return home until after noon. My dad thoroughly enjoyed those Sunday mornings with his friends.

Even after he quit his job, my dad still made the 10 minute drive from our home to the gym. We had been pleading with my dad to stop driving for a while and it always led to an argument. Remember, he was a grown man with grown kids. Why would he want others to tell him not to do something he has been doing his entire adult life? Eventually, we hid the car keys and dealt with the anger, yelling, cursing and him throwing objects at the wall until the day he accepted his inability to drive safely. In hindsight, the man he was then compared to who he'd be five years later was incomparable. Five years later, if you showed him a key he wouldn't know what it was for or what it was called.

After my dad was unable to drive himself to the gym, I would sometimes drive him and we would go together and other times his friends would come pick him up. As time and the disease progressed, the frequency of them coming to get him decreased. My dad was no longer waking up early nor was he as easy to get out of the house as before. He also required a level of observation when he was outside of the home. For these reasons, I understand why the Sunday hangout sessions started to taper off. Granted, I could have done more as well. I could have continued taking him to the gym on those early Sunday mornings, played with him and his friends and gone out with all of them. Honestly, I didn't want to. I wasn't a child but I didn't have the wisdom that I would have a few years later when I began writing this book.

I do wish these friends would have visited my dad at least once a month after their games or throughout the week just to spend some time with him. I wish they would have kept in touch with him instead of disappearing. The worse my father's condition got, the less they came around. As of this writing, I can say that years have gone by without many of these old friends seeing my dad. I can also say that those friends who are spread out across the country stopped calling as well. True friends are those who show up when it's inconvenient. Don't wait until your friend is gone to tell the family, "If there is anything I can do to help, I am here."

I wish his friends knew that while it may have been difficult to see him in that state or awkward to maintain a conversation with him, he still enjoyed their company. Even later on when he would forget people's faces and their names he still felt their connection. He would be upbeat for hours after spending time with a good friend. Sometimes this feeling would last until the next day.

You may have heard that people with Alzheimer's have good days and bad days. I believe that we possess the ability to help alleviate some of the bad days and further improve the good ones. While their mind may not remember you, their soul remembers you. Your friend may not remember you but they need you. Your presence can positively affect their memory and mood for hours after your visit.

I have not seen my friends disappear because of my father's fight with Alzheimer's but I have been surprised by their lack of understanding. It has been my experience that if someone hasn't been personally affected by Alzheimer's, they don't often truly understand the severity of the disease. Rarely would friends ask "How is your dad?" I don't recall a friend ever asking how I'm doing with the situation.

I believe that when a friend is going through something, it is our responsibility as a friend to be there for that person. Otherwise, what is the point of life? What is the point of friends if they don't check up on you during your most trying times? True friends are those who show up when it's inconvenient. Granted, I don't know if they fully understand how serious the disease is. I don't believe they recognize the toll of explaining to someone that the house they woke up in is the house they have lived in for

20 years or the toll of explaining to your father that you're not an intruder-you are his son. The toll of watching someone sleep more, talk less, eat less and struggle to do daily tasks that we take for granted like brushing our teeth, taking a shower and eating.

I love my friends. They have been there for me through a lot and I know if I call them, they will pick up. I know if I show up to their front door, they will let me in-no questions asked. I'm sure many of you have friends like that as well. If you are a friend to someone whose loved one has Alzheimer's, I hope my experience can help you create a support system for your friend.

3
The First Lost Milestone

One heartbreaking experience of Alzheimer's is not being able to fully share milestones with your loved one who is sick. For me, that first milestone was buying my first house. My dad was great with money. He was an investor, had businesses and would often give my friends and I advice on how to manage our money. I am forever grateful for what I learned from him. However, as a teenager, there was only so much I cared to absorb. When it was time to buy my first house, I had to learn a lot on my own.

Learning things on my own wasn't a big deal and everything worked itself out but it was saddening that only two months after my dad's official diagnosis he could no longer help me. Even that early on, he no longer had the mental ability to tell me what to look for when buying a house. He couldn't pass down the minute details a person learns from going through such an experience multiple times. You know, things like what defects to look out for and different ways a bank may try to take advantage of you.

Thinking back, I think I was most disappointed that I couldn't share the moment with my dad. My father, the man who embedded the importance of owning property in me, came to my house multiple times and every time he came over he would ask if it was my house. He would congratulate me and ask me when I bought the house. At the same time I bought my house I had to grieve a loss.

I would have loved for my dad to be a larger part of this journey but he was not able to be. You know when you experience a breakup and then go somewhere and wish you were still with your ex so you could share that moment with them? Throughout the journey of Alzheimer's, that feeling comes up a lot. It's grief. This was the first time I

truly started to grieve the loss of my dad.[1]

---

[1] Watching a loved one progress through Alzheimer's is to grieve multiple deaths. This will be touched on more throughout the book.

4
The Wish We Hate

What is life? Watching someone slowly lose their identity at the mercy of Alzheimer's has caused this question to frequent my mind. I have been watching someone slowly lose themselves while simultaneously seeing that they are still themselves. They still maintain their love and their values. They maintain their true Being-that Being that we are all born with before we are labeled by others and ourselves.

So, what is everything else we identify with apart from labels? I mentioned that the first time I grieved the loss of my dad was when he couldn't help me buy my first home. I grieved losing a part of him that was his identity. Was I beginning to lose the human form of my dad as he slowly started to transform to his true being? Is everything outside of those labels who each and every one of us truly are? I don't know.

My dad often struggled to be present. He was often thinking about the future or regretting the past. He was often deep in thought. Is there an irony to the disease? Do some people refuse the present moment so much and create so much stress for themselves by living in the past, future or both that their body finally has enough and tries to force them to be more present?

Does the subconscious intelligence of the human mind force some people who could never be present to be present? Is this intelligence taking over in a cruel and ironic way? These are all questions I have found myself asking since my father's mental deterioration at the hands of this awful disease.

. . .

As time went on, I would find myself getting annoyed and angry with my dad. Alzheimer's is draining for all parties involved. If you are a caretaker, your life is slowly taken away from you. You may not be able to peacefully sleep at night. You may have to say no to social engagements because you cannot find someone to watch your loved one but if you take them with you, you'll be preoccupied with them rather than enjoying your time. You may constantly be on the lookout for your missing belongings-sometimes large sums of money. Any of these things by themselves could be tolerated if they were isolated incidents. All of these things compounded daily can become exhausting. I will give you a glimpse into a "normal" day.

It is 3 am and you wake up to your mom and dad talking. You find out that your dad woke up, got confused and started to walk around the house looking for your mom (for this scenario, let's say they sleep in different rooms). He finally found your mom because he was shouting her name and woke her up. He was simply confused and did not know where he was. Eventually, you go back to sleep and wake up in the morning to see that the stove is on. Your parents are both sleeping. You realize that at some point during the night your father woke back up, turned on the stove and left it on.

Later, when he finally wakes up, he asks you, "Where are we?" and you remind him that you are at home. He then starts to wander around the kitchen opening cabinets. You ask what he's looking for and he says he is looking for a cup for coffee. Your mom tells him not to worry about it and to have a seat while she brings him a cup. She then has him take his medicine, makes him breakfast and you remind him to drink water.

After breakfast, he tries to go on a walk alone. You know he is no longer able to find his way back home and you go for a walk with him. After you get back, he lays down around the house and relaxes so you go to your room and relax a bit too.

An hour later, you leave your room and you can't find your dad. You look around the house and then realize he is in the garage with the brand new air filter you just placed in the furnace. He claims it is dirty and that it had to be removed because it was no longer effective in trapping the microscopic bugs that are entering his brain and causing him to be confused. You explain to him at length how the filter is clean and new. After five to ten minutes, you finally convince him to give you the air filter so you can go and put it back in its place.

After you come back upstairs from the utility room, you find your dad in your bedroom. On any given day he could just be laying in your bed or taking things out of your room thinking they are his. A couple hours later, your mom asks if you've seen her iPad charger. You tell her you have not, help her look for it and then find it mixed with your dad's belongings. Your mom then asks you if it's okay for her to take a break and go out with her friends. You know she is the main caretaker so you say yes, cancel your plans and stay home with your dad.

While you are home alone with your father, he begins to ask you who you are. You have to show him your ID to try to prove to him that you are his son. Even then, he still doesn't fully believe you. He follows you around the house and has a creepy look of distrust in his eyes that you have never received from him.

Eventually, your mom gets home, he calms down and goes to the restroom to get ready for bed. Shortly after he leaves the restroom you realize that he had locked the door from the inside of the bathroom and then closed it as he exited. You now go to the garage, get the toolbox and proceed to unscrew the doorknob and unlock the door. Finally, you go to sleep.

All of these scenarios have actually happened. This example wasn't from any particular day but specific scenarios from various days that were put together. However, it was not uncommon to have a variation of the aforementioned examples happen daily. I would go as far as saying that what I have just stated could be a typical day for someone with Alzheimer's and their caretakers. Eventually, my dad would get a catheter (more on that later) and that would make everything more difficult.

Going through all of these things daily takes its toll on a person. Furthermore, you are grieving. You are watching someone you love and admire become a shell of their former self. When you are caretaking, it leaves you little room to grieve properly and your emotions may turn to anger and frustration.

Many people wish the disease would hurry up and progress so as to save everyone more pain. A Google search of: "Wishing Alzheimer's patient would die" brings up plenty of results. It is important to remember that these feelings are normal and that it is not the person we want dead but rather the disease, the situation and the pain and suffering that we wish would perish.

5
Animals and Kids

I have mentioned that Alzheimer's requires you to continuously grieve. You are losing a part of your loved one every few months. While they lose characteristics they may have identified themselves with, you realize that their core remains the same. As my father's condition progressed, he was still able to find joy around children and animals.

A family friend had twins who were around five years old. They would light up whenever they saw my dad. They asked about him when he ended up in the hospital. My dad couldn't remember their names nor recognize where he was but he knew they were children and treated them with the respect, kindness and patience that children deserve. Whenever my dad spoke with his nephews' and nieces' children overseas, he would light up, change his tone and tell the children how smart, beautiful and amazing they were. It was in my dad's core-his Being-to look out for those who were younger, those who were vulnerable.

My father taught me a lesson that I have tried my best to live out: he always told me to fight for those who cannot fight for themselves; he taught me to be a voice for the voiceless. He wasn't just talking about people. My father was a firm believer that animals have an intelligence that was on par or more advanced than ours. He would always tell me that non-human animals know way more than we think they do. For a long time, I was scared of most animals. This stemmed from my mom's fear of dogs and cats. I did not see the beautiful compassion and intelligence that animals possess until I met my dog, Shiraz.

Three and a half months before my dad was officially diagnosed with Alzheimer's, Shiraz came into our lives. Shiraz has played an important role in supporting both my parents and myself during our journey with Alzheimer's disease. I believe he was heaven-sent.

The day Shiraz came into our lives, I made a spontaneous trip to a local shelter. I had no intention of leaving with a dog. Many people had passed up on him over the weekend. A staff member told me they were surprised he was still there on that Sunday afternoon. It was all either a big coincidence or someone was looking out for Shiraz, myself and my family (which Shiraz is now a part of).

When my dad first met Shiraz, they would cuddle together and Shiraz would go to my dad for pets. There was nobody he cuddled harder with or preferred to go to more for a relaxing scratch or massage than my dad. During the beginning stages of the disease-when my dad still remembered directions-he would take Shiraz for walks when I was at work and for a long time he joined Shiraz and I for walks in the neighborhood and throughout the city. After many of these walks, my dad would thank me. He thoroughly enjoyed being outside, getting exercise and being with Shiraz and I.

Some days my dad was too depressed or simply not feeling well enough to get out of bed. On these days, I would send Shiraz into my dad's room and he would just cuddle with my dad until he got up. Whenever my dad would get frustrated from not remembering or become anxious, I would direct his attention to Shiraz. All I had to do was say something simple like, "Look at how cute he is while he's sleeping" or, "Shiraz wants you to sit by him and pet him. Can you do that?"

These redirections often worked. Shiraz's energy, presence and joy had a huge effect on my dad's well-being. It was amazing. Looking back, it seems almost magical. Shiraz didn't have to do anything other than just be. They would often fall asleep together on the couch and as my dad was dozing off you could still see him gently petting him.

Shiraz had a huge influence on my mom as well. The stress of being the main caretaker for someone can be taxing. It can be physically, mentally and spiritually draining. Shiraz offset the low times with his presence. He made my mom melt. She went from being terrified of dogs to buying him toys, cuddling with him, helping me make his food, talking to him and constantly feeding him snacks. No matter how low my mom was feeling, when she saw Shiraz, her mood would instantly change; she would become happy and present and tell him how much she loves and adores him.

I believe my parents needed Shiraz. They needed his love, energy and presence. Throughout some of the most difficult times, he was a ray of joy. When everything else seemed to be falling apart, a look at him would remind us that there is still joy in this world.

Four years after my dad's official diagnosis my dad sometimes forgot my name but he almost always remembered that my dog's name was Shiraz. It was incredible because they met while my dad had the disease. My dad had never known Shiraz before he showed symptoms of Alzheimer's and yet, here we were. While my dad struggled at times to put coherent sentences together, he still remembered the name of our best friend.

6
Who Are You?

As soon as my dad was diagnosed with Alzheimer's, I wondered what it would feel like when he forgot who I am. The first time he forgot my name was during a frigid winter night in Minnesota. It was one of those nights when the sun sets before 5 pm, barely gets above the tree lines and the snow on the ground absorbs much of the noise making for a quiet night.

Every morning before work, I would drop Shiraz off with my parents so he wouldn't be alone. After work, I would go over to their house, eat, hang out for a couple hours and then go back to my house with Shiraz. Whenever it was time to go, I would put on my shoes in the entryway between the garage and the kitchen while my parents said their goodbyes to us. One night as I was putting my shoes on, my dad started to talk to me in the distinct way he talked to his friends and cousins. This caught me off guard. He said it was good to see me and that I should come over more often and not be such a stranger. My mom and I looked at each other confused. She turned to my dad and asked him who I was. He said, "What do you mean? That's [my cousin] Saeed."

My mom looked at him and responded, "Are you kidding? Look at him, that's your son." My dad couldn't believe it. He looked at me then back at my mom then back at me and said, "Get out of here. Y'all are just messing with me. That's not Omid."

At this point, I could feel my emotions starting to take over my body. I was about to cry. I quickly said bye without trying to convince my dad that I was his son. I got in my car. I cried. I felt sad and angry. I eventually gathered myself enough to begin the 15 minute drive home but I could not stop intermittently crying during the short trip.

When I arrived home, I ran to my bed and wept. My father not remembering me was something new I had to grieve.

It was not like I had just gotten a haircut. It hadn't been weeks since my dad had seen me. I was there almost every day. Earlier that day he seemed to know who I was. That night he had me confused with someone else.

The interesting thing is that after this happened, many months went by before he thought I was someone else again. This is very typical of Alzheimer's and why it may be hard to tell if someone has Alzheimer's during the early stages of the disease. A person will forget something one minute and then remember it the next. They may forget their address one day and then remember it the next 100 times you ask them. Of course, as the disease progresses, the frequency of forgetting increases while remembering decreases. Eventually, remembering becomes surprising and forgetting becomes the norm.

While it was nice that my dad didn't end up completely forgetting me that winter night, it was an example of the many reminders we get that Alzheimer's has no cure. Once a person with Alzheimer's forgets something, you know they will forget it again at some point in the future. When they forget something or you have to repeat the same thing multiple times in 10 minutes, it can become exhausting.

I wish I would have gotten less frustrated with my dad during these moments. I wish that I would have taken advantage of the moments that were mentally and emotionally draining because eventually my dad couldn't even hold a conversation. I outlined what a typical day for someone with Alzheimer's may be like and explained how when that gets compounded day after day, it truly is exhausting. When I look back at pictures from just one year ago and see how much more aware he was of everything, I wish I would have powered through that exhaustion and frustration. I missed out on my chances to play basketball with him one last time; play one last game of backgammon; have one last conversation about his childhood.

I understand how difficult it is to enjoy the moment when you are a caretaker. In the moments when you feel home-bound and feel like you're missing out on doing all these things you had planned to do-often with the person who has the disease-it can be extremely difficult to just enjoy the moment with the person who has Alzheimer's. You may even feel resentful.

As the disease progresses, the moments we are able to share are not like the moments that we used to have. An Alzheimer patient is able to communicate less and less over time and they eventually end up needing a level of care similar to a baby. You can't interact with them the same way or do the same things you used to. As I write this, it is a good reminder to embrace these changing moments, adapt to them and take advantage of them before they too are taken away.

• • •

When I was a teenager, my dad would tell me stories about his childhood and his journey as an adult. He would sprinkle in life lessons here and there. As a kid, I was concerned about my own personal issues and just getting through school rather than conversing with him and truly grasping the wisdom he was imparting on me in those moments. Eventually, I went away to college and didn't live at home. When I was ready to meet my dad at his level and deepen our relationship, it was too late. Even the foundation of who he was came into question for me.

There would be times when someone would say something and my dad would disagree for no reason. During the early and middle stages of the disease, he did this a lot with my mom and as someone who had now experienced adult relationships, I could understand how this could become exhausting over time. Other times, he would make a comment and couldn't be convinced otherwise.

For example, we could be eating lunch as a family and he would make up an elaborate story about how one of his close friends tried to recently steal from him and begin to vehemently curse their name. Was he always this stubborn? Did he really have so much mistrust and discontent for his closest friends? The weird part was that those whom he had never trusted (like his mother-in-law), he now adored.

I would get upset in these moments because I would begin to wonder if this is who he always was. I would question if he just hid this side of himself from me when I was a child. I would argue with him. I would ask him how he could say something like that about someone or ask him why he couldn't just swallow his pride and agree with what we were presenting him. He would tell me to be quiet and to mind my own business and I would tell him that this was my business because I wanted to know who he really was.

In truth, I was wrong. I was hurt. I was emotional and I let my emotions take over. Certain negative traits that my dad had as the disease progressed were new. Other ones would just become more prevalent and extreme as the disease progressed. I wanted to know if this person was really who my dad always was but looking back, I don't believe it was.

I mentioned earlier that Alzheimer's forces you to slowly watch someone lose their identity and withdraw from the labels they have given themselves and that society has given to them. I stated that they also maintain their love, their values and their true being. I still believe this to be true. I believe while they retain their core values and their true Being, their brain is still trying to create labels and identities to help them make sense of the world; to make them still feel part of the world they have always known. It allows them to remember something even if that something never happened or isn't real.

7

History Repeats

My father left Iran around the age of 29. He told me that it was always his dream to live somewhere else. My father was proud to be Iranian but he had this feeling inside of him that he needed to be somewhere else. Unlike my father, I never thought about leaving my birthplace of Minnesota. I was a diehard Minnesota Timberwolves fan, always talked about how Minneapolis was the greatest city in the country and thought I would be there forever.

When I was 26, I took a spontaneous trip to Atlanta. Like Shiraz, it was not planned and not something that was on my radar. I fell in love with the city and began to tell my friends that I wanted to eventually move to Atlanta.

Around the time of this trip, my feelings about Minnesota were beginning to shift. I began to deeply dread winters. I began to crave being in a new city that was more connected to the world. As the years progressed, this desire to leave and my wish to never experience a full Minnesota winter again became stronger. When I turned 30, many experiences in my life had come full circle and the opportunity to move to Atlanta presented itself. I had nothing holding me back… except my father's Alzheimer's.

Around the time my dad came to the United States, his father was in the middle stages of Alzheimer's. My grandfather eventually passed away from the disease before I was born and while my dad was attending university in the United States. I believe this always took a toll on my dad.

My father was very open about his past and often told me stories but he never talked about what my grandpa was like when he was battling Alzheimer's. I never realized that until I just wrote it. It makes sense, though. Why would he want to talk about his father's battle with the disease? Why would he want to relive the feeling of being on the other side of the world while his dad was slowly dying.

• • •

I seized the aforementioned opportunity and moved to Georgia. My father was in the middle stages of Alzheimer's when I made this move just like his father was when he moved. There are times I feel like my move was selfish. I completely understand my dad leaving Iran while his dad was sick.

He had the opportunity to move to the other side of the world and that wasn't an opportunity that was always going to be there. I feel selfish because it is relatively easy to move within your own country; you can just pack up your car and drive, which is exactly what I ended up doing. I packed up my little Nissan Versa, put Shiraz's bed in the back and we ventured south. I left my mom to take care of my dad. I left my dad. I took Shiraz away from both of them. I mentioned earlier that I didn't appreciate the moments I had with my father when he was progressing through the disease because I was too stressed. Well, instead of moving I could have simply stayed and enjoyed those moments. At the same time, I am not sure if I would have had that realization if I didn't move. Moving gave me clarity. It brought me an inner peace that I had never felt before. Moving did not take away my pain though.

Some people may read this and be the sibling who has put everything on hold to take care of a parent while their brothers and sisters are following their own paths. Others may be the siblings who are following their own path while their brother or sister stays home and takes care of their parent. A few years ago I would have said the latter are wrong and selfish. However, I've learned things aren't always so black and white.

I was in a deep depression before I moved. There were many traumas I had experienced in Minnesota and every time winter came around, my pain was amplified and I would be crippled by depression. I went to therapy and it helped me a lot. At some point though, I knew I had to do more.

Even as I list my reasons for leaving, I cannot help but feel an immense guilt for leaving my parents. I was 30 years old. I wanted to be there for my dad. I wanted to support my mom. I wanted to live my own life. Where is the line between selfishness and self-care?

What if I never moved and I was stuck in Minnesota for another 10 years taking care of my dad and fell in a deeper hole of depression? What if, after my dad passes away, I have a deep sense of regret for not having stayed with him? The way we react to the disease often leads to self-questioning and internal conflicts. As the child of immigrants, I feel this sense of entitlement. This feeling that my parents sacrificed everything so that I could do everything they couldn't. My dad always told me to do what made me happy. He always told me to follow my heart. My dad was my greatest cheerleader.

As I started to go back-and-forth between Minneapolis and Atlanta to find a place to live and as he saw me packing, my dad would ask me not to leave. I would bring up the fact that he moved far away when his dad was ill too. He never seemed to fully grasp what I meant. In hindsight, it was probably an insensitive thing to say.

I left Minnesota around 5 am on Thanksgiving Eve, 2020. My dad was sleeping when I was about to leave and part of me wanted to leave without saying goodbye because I knew I would break down. I knew saying bye to him would be difficult because even if I saw him alive again, he would not be the same person. I would have to grieve the loss of another, or multiple, parts of him. After I packed up my car, I went upstairs, woke him up and just cried. I sobbed. He was laying on his back and I put my face into his shoulders and just broke down.

He had Alzheimer's and was just woken up. He had no idea what was going on but my emotional breakdown made him break down. He began to cry and ask what was happening. I told him I was leaving and he just kept crying. Shiraz noticed this, jumped on the bed and began to comfort my dad. Knowing that he was also saying goodbye to Shiraz made me cry even more.

I have had to step away from writing this book at times because it can be emotionally draining to relive these memories. Writing the previous paragraph was the first time I actually broke down and cried while writing this book. When I was younger, we would visit Iran every few years. Every time we left, I would cry hysterically because I was essentially saying goodbye to my entire family. I never knew if I'd ever go back and there was also a chance someone would die before my next visit.

The last time I went was 16 years ago. The visit before that, my great grandma died after I left. Before that, my great grandpa died. And the visit before that, my grandma died after I left. More recently, an uncle, two great-uncles, two aunts and my maternal grandparents passed away over the last four years. Those goodbyes 16 years ago were final. This time, I was leaving my home in Minnesota and I knew I was going to lose part of my dad before I saw him again. I cried like I was leaving Iran.

8

The Trip Back

I was enjoying my first few months in Georgia. No snow, daily walks with Shiraz and exploring a new area made for a good winter. In late February, my parents flew to San Diego to visit and stay with their friends for a week. I kept in daily contact with my mom after I moved. She told me that during their trip, my dad would wake up in the middle of the night and wander into other people's rooms. He had no idea where he was. This made it difficult for my mom to sleep. She was always worried about him walking into someone else's room and waking them up. My mother also told me that at times my father would go into the bathroom for 20-30 minutes.

When they were flying from San Diego back to Minneapolis, my dad had to use the restroom. After 10 minutes, my mom began to worry. The bathroom was empty and she could not find my dad. She asked a flight attendant for help locating him. Not long after, they found him. He upgraded himself and he was taking a nap in first class. Sometimes, all you can do is laugh. Sometimes, you have to laugh.

Around noon on the day after my parents got back to Minnesota, I was on the phone with my mom and asked her to hand the phone to my dad. He was completely unresponsive. My mom kept saying, "Get up and speak to your son. It's your son. Say 'hello.'" He wouldn't budge and my mom told me that he felt very cold. I got worried and suggested she take him to a doctor.

Eight hours went by and I hadn't heard a word from my mom. Shiraz and I were on a walk and I decided to call her. She told me my dad was in the hospital. Her reason for not telling me was that she did not want to worry me, as if I wouldn't find out. She told me that when he got to the hospital, his temperature was 91 degrees and his blood pressure put him in a hypertensive crisis. In addition to this, his creatinine[2] level was 19.03 mg/dl[3] and the standard range is .70-1.30 mg/dl. My dad had kidney failure and the likely cause and his subsequent hospitalization were due to a mix of medications he was on.

My mom—against my sister's advice and urging—gave my dad sleeping pills when they were in San Diego. This did not mix well with the regular medication he was on and led to his kidney issues. To put it bluntly and very simply, my dad had urine backed up in his body and was not able to go to the bathroom. All that time he spent in the bathroom at their friends' house in San Diego may have had a reason behind it.

My sister and I believe my father was closer to dying at that moment than we all realized. When I heard that he was in the hospital, I decided I had to go back

---

[2] Creatinine is a waste product that is removed through the kidneys.
[3] mg/dl is the milligrams of creatinine to a deciliter of blood

home. Just three and a half months earlier, I was driving down to Georgia. The morning after my dad was admitted into the hospital, I drove back to Minnesota... far sooner than I anticipated.

My dad was at Hennepin County Medical Center in downtown Minneapolis for a week while he recovered. He was in surprisingly good spirits and oftentimes, he thought he was home and the rest of the family was just upstairs. Unfortunately, this event led to my dad having to wear a catheter for the rest of his life.

Under normal circumstances, a catheter is not ideal. When a person has Alzheimer's and forgets after one minute what is attached to his body, a catheter can break a caregiver. When my father was wheelchaired out of the hospital and I pulled up with my car to take him home, he was not happy. I think he was confused. He had been in the hospital for a week and now he likely had no idea what was going on.

When he got in the car, he still appeared angry. I asked what was wrong and he would just ask where my mom was and what was attached to his leg. I explained to him numerous times during our 30 minute car ride that my mom couldn't come to the hospital because of a disease called Covid-19 and that she was at home waiting for him.

Eventually, as is often the case, I just shortened my response and told him that she was at home watching Shiraz. As far as the catheter was concerned, I had to keep telling him that we just left the hospital and that the catheter had to stay in place because it was helping his body. It is one thing to have to answer the same questions over and over but it becomes more exhausting when you don't recognize the person you are talking to.

When we finally arrived home, Shiraz ran to the car and greeted my dad with the excitement and enthusiasm that are stereotypical of a dog. The fact that he hadn't seen my dad in over three months only added to his excitement.

My dad didn't even seem to notice. He didn't say hi to Shiraz. He just tried to throw his catheter and kept saying that he wanted to die.

From that moment on, taking care of my dad became more difficult. Before, we only had to worry about him wandering around the house and screaming for my mom in the middle of the night. Now, we had to worry about him taking out his catheter too. Most nights he would detach the catheter from its bag. This would cause a mess and my mom would end up washing his sheets almost every morning.

During the day, my father wore a smaller bag that could be wrapped around his leg. My mom would make sure he had on pants covering the catheter to make it as inconspicuous as possible. Out of sight and out of mind was our only option. At some point throughout each day, he would notice the bag and unhook it. Sometimes he would even try to throw the bag while it was still attached to him.

One time he took off the bag in the backyard and threw it into the woods.

We tried to supervise him as much as we could and stop him before he took out the catheter. Every time we stopped him we had to explain why he was wearing it. My mom even got a note from a nurse to show my father whenever he didn't believe us. The problem was that we couldn't watch him in the middle of the night and at times, he would go take a nap during the day and then we'd come to find out that he took out the catheter again.

We made it a habit to not sleep until he went to bed. My mom made sure to tuck him in every night. The only issue was that he would almost always get up in the middle of the night and, as mentioned earlier, mess with the catheter. When he felt wet, he would say that he must have spilled water on himself. This even happened one time in my mom's friend's car. You can imagine how my mom felt.

He never understood the catheter and never learned to live with it.

9

I Said This Would Never Happen

After three and a half weeks in Minnesota, I went back to Georgia. I kept up the daily calls with my mom. She was more stressed than ever. She would tell me that my dad was harder to deal with than ever before. In chapter four I explained the cruel irony that may have triggered my dad's Alzheimer's. In addition to everything I've previously mentioned, another powerful force that may have led to him becoming sick may have been my mom.

My mom told me on more than one occasion that she prayed for my dad to get sick. She didn't specifically wish Alzheimer's on him but she prayed he would get sick and needy so he would be more grateful for her. After seeing my maternal grandpa die unexpectedly and knowing the constant stress he was under from my grandma, I further believe that my mom may have had some part in my dad becoming sick. My grandpa had a stroke and was not well taken care of after. I believe if he would have been with any other relative or in a more positive environment, he wouldn't have died so suddenly. The stress and negative energy that is spewed at a person on a daily basis by someone they live with can do serious damage.

Look at kids... We often say they're a product of their environment. If they are sensitive to their environment then I believe that spouses, who spend so much time together and share a home together, must feel and be impacted by each other's energy.

I can imagine some people would find it surprising for someone to talk about their mother and grandmother in this way. As I mentioned earlier: history repeats; some children become everything they hated about their mother, father or both and then treat others the way they were treated and the way they saw others treated. I don't believe the things my mom did for my dad after he got sick were out of love. I believe they were out of guilt. I'll touch more on how she treated my dad later in this book.

• • •

It is normal for Alzheimer's patients to get paranoid and anxious and this often leads to anger. They become paranoid because they don't know who anyone is and forget where they are. They don't trust anyone. My dad thought my mom was cheating on him. He thought people who came over were going to hurt or steal from him. You can imagine how all of this anxiety, stress, paranoia and sadness that stem from memory loss can cause someone to become angry.

My dad would get frustrated and throw things. He never directed any objects or physical attacks towards anyone. The absence of physical violence was who my dad always was. Despite everything that was changing, this deeply held value to not harm others remained. It didn't mean we weren't scared of him doing something unpredictable though.

People with Alzheimer's can become anxious because their short term memory is either fading or gone. This causes them to go into a cycle of compulsive thinking where they try to remember what they just did and what they need to do next. Imagine waking up one day and not recognizing your wife or your house and then trying to think about what is outside of the room you just woke up in. Imagine leaving the room and trying to predict what each door leads to and worrying that you are alone in an unfamiliar environment. Imagine attempting to recognize if every person you see in this seemingly foreign building is a friend or foe.

My father even forgot that his parents passed away decades ago. He used to ask his brothers and sisters in Iran how his parents were doing. This caught them off guard. They would say, "They've been gone for a long time," and my dad would lose it. It was as if he was reliving the experience of his parents' death all over again.

They quickly realized—and my mom made sure to let everyone know—that when he asked how his parents are doing, they should simply state that his parents are doing well. When he asked to speak to them, they would tell him that his parents were old and not good with technology or that they were sleeping. Lying sucks. In a situation like this though, we all had to be part of the lie to prevent my dad from reliving that pain. If we told him the truth, he would have relived those deaths multiple times per week.

• • •

The combination of outbursts, being woken up in the middle of the night and the stress of having to clean up multiple times a day because my dad pulled out his catheter understandably took a toll on my mom. I always told her that since she was the main caretaker, I would support her decisions. One day the compounded pressure, stress, anxiety and pain became too much for my mom and she began to tour places to move my dad.

I can't stress that word *compounded* enough. Dealing with something for a day, week or even a month can be manageable. Dealing with something multiple times a day for years will eventually take its toll on someone.

Shampooing the carpet because urine spilled on it and having to wash the sheets may not be a big deal for one day but when it happens every day, you build anxiety because you're always worried about the next time it will occur. When you can no longer go to parties and enjoy a nice night out with your husband, you grieve. With the grieving, you may also grow resentment. At the same time that you are losing someone, you are also having to take care of them and constantly monitor them.

It's like taking care of a big kid. You have to take them with you everywhere. At times, you have to redirect them. You may have to change their clothes if they have an accident. You may have to help feed them. You may have to go home early because they are growing anxious due to the fact that they don't remember where they are and who is around them. Alzheimer's causes caretakers to lose a lot of their freedom. The patient becomes a burden.

With all of this going on, my mom could no longer be an effective caretaker. She was becoming ill, both mentally and physically. Resentment towards my father was growing. One day she called me and told me she was looking for a memory care facility for my father. My only advice was to trust her intuition.

She went to a few facilities she didn't like. The problem was that since my dad was on medicaid there were only so many places we could afford to take him. She finally found a place she liked and my sister and her husband toured the place and said they approved too. I trusted them. With all this decision making, it is heartbreaking to think that my dad had no input. He went on these tours with my mom but by that point his Alzheimer's had gotten so bad that he was rarely aware of where he was or what was going on around him.

Imagine one day you wake up in the house that you bought and you don't know that it is the last time you will ever be in that house again. Even though my father woke up most mornings not knowing where he was or who we were, I truly believe his soul knew that was home. His energy was spread out throughout the house. He had been living there for 22 years. His children grew up there. Now, in April of 2021, almost five years after my dad sent me a text telling me he was going to end up like Pat Summit, he was moving to a new "home."

• • •

I was always adamant against putting my parents in a nursing home. I believed that family took care of family and that putting somebody in a memory care facility or nursing home was often a lazy and selfish decision. I was obviously wrong. I hadn't thought about the plethora of circumstances that may lead to a family putting a loved one in a care facility. For us, these circumstances included: me moving, my sister being pregnant and being preoccupied with her job and family and my mom not having the mental or physical capabilities to take care of my dad.

Even though I moved away and, as I just explained, it was wrong for me to judge others, I still expected more from my mom. My mother has dealt with mental health issues since I was a child. She tried to mask these issues with prescribed drugs and she refused to see a therapist. Her response to seeing a therapist was almost always, "Why should I if you don't?" When I'd tell her I was in therapy she would make remarks like, "Well, it obviously isn't working for you so why should I go?" As time progressed and my mental health improved, her response evolved to just ignoring me any time I recommended therapy.

I believe my mother's mental health also had a terrible effect on her physical health. She was always in pain and had multiple surgeries over the years. Every time she had pain, the doctors said they didn't know the cause but they always ended up doing surgery to alleviate the pain. First she had surgery on her shoulder. The pain disappeared for a year and then manifested further down her arm. The next place she had pain was her elbow. Then her wrist. Doctors told her she had carpal tunnel so she had surgery on her wrist to alleviate that pain.

Every new pain manifested quicker than the last one. Less than a year after her wrist surgery, she had pain in her hand. As of this writing, her pain is concentrated in her stomach. My belief is that all or most of this pain is a result of stress. I believe not taking care of her mental health led to these physical ailments which eventually led to her not being able to be an effective caretaker for my father. She lacked the physical capabilities and the mental capacity. In other words: she was at her breaking point and maybe I shouldn't have expected as much as I did from her.

I understand that she was under immense stress. She was losing her husband and as I've mentioned throughout the book, being a caretaker is exhausting for many reasons that just keep compounding. Do I believe that therapy will allow someone to be the perfect caretaker? No, but I wish she would have tried. I wish she would have taken her marriage oath more seriously. That's why sometimes I'm more disappointed in her than everyone else. My parents were never good for each other. They were in a loveless marriage and divorce was the right answer. Divorce could have led to both of them finding someone who would truly love them and better care for them. Again though, who am I to judge? I haven't walked in their shoes so maybe my beliefs are just bullshit.

Even with therapy, being around my father was hard. Watching him die in front of me was hard. I would still get upset with him. Therapy did help me process my emotions and gave me tools to be a better caretaker though. Through therapy I was able to realize that when I was mad at my dad, I was actually mad at his condition. I was mad at the disease. Therapy helped me accept what was happening. Therapy gave me an outlet and a safe space. I was lucky to have a great therapist from the beginning and I know that some therapists are not great. If someone has had a bad experience with a therapist, I hope they are able to find a more qualified individual because I believe we can only do so much for others if we are not doing enough for ourselves. Sometimes therapy helps us realize what we need for ourselves because-ironically-we are too in our own heads.

Even with therapy, caretaking is exhausting. It is both mentally and physically draining. Without proper mental and physical care, you can imagine how much harder the day-to-day stressors are to handle. There is a mental and physical stress to changing sheets and shampooing the carpet every day. There is a mental and physical stress to being woken up in the middle of the night because someone is looking for you. There is a mental and physical stress to not being able to fall asleep because you are worried about what the person being cared for is going to do tomorrow. In addition to all of this, the more mental stress you carry with you, the more you will begin to feel that tension in your body and that tension may eventually become physical pain. That pain can then lead to a deteriorated mental state. It can become a vicious cycle.

All of this makes it understandable why a family would have to put someone in a care facility. I had done a 180 from what I always believed and told my mother to do what she thought was best, even if that was putting my father in a memory care facility. Going through

Alzheimer's is not easy and has often made me wonder what could have been done to prevent it. Life-changing decisions are being made while the world keeps moving and my human mind is trying to figure out the gray in a situation that is neither black nor white.

• • •

After my dad was placed in a new "home," my mom would video call me every time she visited him. She would tell me the place is clean, the staff is nice and that my dad seems to be enjoying himself and the food. My sister confirmed this. I believed them. About a month and a half after my dad moved out of my childhood home, Shiraz and I made the 17 hour drive back up to Minnesota.

The first time I drove up to Minnesota, I was not looking forward to it. I had only been in Georgia for four months, it was spring and the flowers were about to bloom and I was not looking forward to another 1,000 mile one-way trip. This time, however, I was excited. I was excited to see my family and friends. I was also excited for Shiraz and I to get out of our one bedroom apartment and have some more room to run around and play together. I was excited for summer in the land of 10,000 lakes. I was excited to see my dad.

10
Home

I drove my regular route: 10 hours to Chicago where I crashed at a friend's house and then about seven more hours of driving until I got home. My mom had my favorite Persian food ready for me when I arrived. A lentil and eggplant based stew called *gheymeh* with tahdig (crispy persian rice). I was home. I was tired but I was relaxed and Shiraz was happy. Shiraz was also curious. He was curious as to where my dad was. He sniffed all over the house looking for him. It was weird being home and not having my dad there. Like, really weird. You spend your entire life growing up in the same house as someone and then when you're older, you visit them in that same house. One day, they are just not there anymore.

After that last paragraph, I did not add a word to this book for over a month. This trip was difficult.

• • •

When I woke up the next morning, I got ready to go visit my dad. Shiraz came with and because of Covid protocols, dogs were temporarily not allowed in the building. So, my mom went into the building and got my dad while I waited outside with Shiraz. When my dad came outside, he seemed to lack emotion. He just stood there. Shiraz was losing his mind. He was barking at my dad. Jumping on him. Shiraz was so excited to see my dad and my dad just stood there frozen. After a few barks and jumps we told my dad that Shiraz was trying to say hi and he said, "Oh. Hey Shiraz," while offering him a few pets. Even after this interaction, he still did not have the usual joy he possessed when he saw Shiraz. He didn't have the usual joy he possessed when he saw me.

My mom brought my dad some leftover gheymeh and they went inside so my dad could eat while Shiraz and I went to a rose garden near Lake Harriet in Minneapolis. At that moment, I didn't think much about my dad's reaction to Shiraz. I mean, why would I? How much was I supposed to dwell on it? Sometimes I wish I would have been more mindful. I wish that after my dad's reaction to seeing us, I sat and focused my energy on how it felt seeing him standing outside like a zombie. I believe doing so would have allowed me to process my emotions rather than having them build and wait to have fuel poured over them.

Eventually, Shiraz and I went back to my mom and dad. We all sat in the courtyard together for about 15 minutes and then my mom, Shiraz and I left because it was too hot for Shiraz. I felt bad that I couldn't stay longer but I was going to be back the next day, a Thursday.

• • •

Thursday morning I was tired and had to resolve an issue with my car so I took my car to the mechanic and relaxed in the morning. I went to visit my dad in the afternoon and when I got to his room, he was sleeping. My knocking woke him up but he was happier to see me than he was the day before. One of the first things I noticed when I walked in was that the floor was sticky. Why was his floor sticky? Why were they not cleaning it more? I hated that he was there. Anyway, there wasn't much to do in his room so I suggested that we go for a walk.

About five minutes into our walk my dad asked me where my mom was. I told him that she was at home watching my dog. A couple minutes went by and he asked the same question and I gave the same answer. Every few minutes he was asking the same question. I kept trying to keep him present. I would point at birds, squirrels and trees and encourage him to look at them. He always loved nature. My plan did not work too well. It felt like even when I was talking about something else, he was worried about where my mom was. At one point I was talking about my own life and he responded by again asking where my mom was. I was disappointed and encouraged him to stop worrying and to "Listen to what I, your son, am telling you about my life."

It was as if he would understand for a second. He would look at a bird, squirrel or tree for a second. Then, he would go right back to worrying. The memory loss created severe anxiety which, in this instance, was fueled by him trying to find out where his partner was. This anxiety is a common side-effect of Alzheimer's. It makes sense. They don't know what is going on and no amount of explaining that everything is okay will make the situation better because they will immediately forget what you say. Ironically, they may not forget what they are anxious about.

We walked around for a while and then went inside and hung out. My dad was tired and laid down. I could tell he wanted to sleep but I could not tell him that I was going to leave. Doing so would lead to him asking to come with me. I told him I was going to go and get water from my car and that I would be right back. He believed me. I left. I hated having to lie like that but as the next day would show, I really had no choice.

The next day, I left home around noon to go visit my dad. I ordered two pizzas from Punch Pizza in Minneapolis to enjoy with him. When I arrived around 1 pm, his catheter was full. I calmly asked a nurse to empty it but I was very upset. As I mentioned earlier, his floor was sticky and now his catheter was full. This was exactly why I didn't want my father to be away from home. While I understood the reasoning for him being there, I was not happy with the result. I was not happy that my mom and sister talked the place up like it was great. It wasn't. It was depressing.

My perception may have been influenced by the fact that the whole situation was personal for me. My perception could have been tainted by the fact that I was not happy my dad was there. My personal emotions about my dad's health and situation may have made the entire place seem more depressing. I am not sure. Whatever it was, it sucked and every negative thing-like a sticky floor or full catheter-seemed to justify my feelings.

After the nurse emptied the catheter, we went to the patio and enjoyed the pizza. It was another hot summer day in Minnesota. The sun was out and it was 90 degrees but my dad insisted on sitting in the sun[4]. He was always cold. The worse his Alzheimer's got, the more he would feel cold. After we ate our pizza, we went for a walk to a nearby garden and back. After we got back, I told him I was going to go to the corner store and buy us some water. He was okay with this and trusted that I would come back. After I

---

[4] I recommend having plenty of water for Alzheimer's patience and looking out for signs of heat exhaustion when outside on hot days. They may not be able to communicate that they are hot.

came back, we hung out for a little bit. I sat around watching local TV while he took a nap for about an hour and then we did the only thing there was to do… we went for another walk. After about five or six hours of being there, I told my dad I was going to go get something from my car. This time, he didn't believe me. He knew I was going to leave. He begged me to take him with me. That's when one of the most heartbreaking moments of my life occurred.

My dad snapped out of his Alzheimer's for a few minutes. He looked me in the eyes with tears crawling down his face. He said, "This isn't how a person is supposed to live. Put yourself in my shoes. Please take me home. Take me with you."

I told my dad that him leaving was not in my control. I reminded him that my mom had to make that decision and that she wasn't capable of providing proper care for him. He continued begging me to help him get out of that place. I told him that I would do everything in my power to get him home. He looked me in the eyes and made me promise him. At that moment, I made the promise and I meant it deep in my heart. I wanted nothing more than to get my dad out of there. This calmed him down a lot. He laid down and allowed me to leave. I got in my car and cried before driving home.

• • •

I was pissed at my mom. How could she allow my dad to stay in such a place? How could she lie to me about the conditions there? How could she disavow her marriage? In the few weeks that preceded my arrival to Minnesota, my mom would tell me how she felt guilty for having my dad in a "home." When I got back to the house I grew up in, I let her know that I was upset with her. I told her that she deserved to feel guilty because that is not how one should leave someone they made the commitment of marriage to.

The next day, my feelings were the same. I told her she was wrong for putting him in that nursing home and that I would fight to get him out. I told her everything my dad told me and she didn't say anything. My relationship with my mother has rarely been a good one. I had to go to therapy to forgive her for many of the things she had done to me. This is not to say that I was right in this situation.

Decades of pent up emotion were mixed with the gasoline of seeing my dad in tears while standing on a sticky floor with a catheter attached to his leg to ignite my frustrations. I admit, I could have handled the situation better. I could have gone back to my mom's house, told my mom what my dad told me and told her that I wanted to work with her to find a better solution. I was wrong in how I handled the situation and I believe my mom was wrong for what she did next.

It was around 8:30 am the following day and my feelings still had not changed. My mom was preparing stuff for lunch and I told her I didn't want anything she was making. No swearing. No yelling. Nothing more than me saying I wanted nothing from her. She then left the house and sent a text a few minutes later saying that I had until 10 am to leave or she would call the police. She kicked Shiraz and I out. I left. I drove back to Georgia with a pitstop in Chicago to stay with my friend.

While I was in Chicago, my mom's best friend called me. She had spoken with my mom and she encouraged me to just stay away for a day or two and then go back and talk to my mom. She also offered to facilitate the conversation. I told her I was in Chicago and driving back home to Georgia and she was shocked. My mom's friend told me to go back to Minnesota so we could work things out. It was obvious to me that my mom had spoken to her friend. It was obvious to me that my mom was not going to call the cops. I was upset and hurt her feelings so she did what she always does when she feels attacked or threatened: she tried to hurt me.

I believe my mom thought I would leave, go to a friend's house in Minnesota and then she would have her friend mediate so we could work the problem out. Instead, a couple days later I was back in Georgia. For me, the worst part wasn't that she kicked me out. It was that I was now over 1,000 miles away from my dad.

I believe a lot of emotional pain that I was carrying surfaced after watching my dad beg me to take him home. Throughout this entire unfortunate journey, I wish my mother would have been more empathetic towards me watching my dad slowly die. From the time my dad started showing signs of Alzheimer's up until the time he was placed in the memory care facility, my mom made fun of my dad. She would talk bad about him. At times, she even questioned if he was faking his Alzheimer's. She would immediately change her demeanor when he walked into a room. She would change her tone when talking to him. She would make fun of him in front of guests.

Some of the things she would rag on my dad for were traits that I possess like looking out the window at nature. Yes, I am their child and I am not aware of everything that happened within their marriage but I know that the way I saw my mom treat my dad while he was sick affected me deeply. After my dad was placed in the care facility, my mom mentioned that she was able to love him again. She did not feel the burden she had been feeling for so many years. I believe this is partially true but I believe her love stemmed from guilt.

11
Video Chats

In less than a week I had driven to Minneapolis and back down to Atlanta. My maternal uncle in Germany started getting in frequent contact with me. My mom's brother kept telling me to call my mom; telling me that she is upset and wants to move past what happened. From my perspective, that's what my mom always wants to do. She rarely acknowledges what happened. She rarely initiates a conversation after an argument and instead ignores me and waits for me to apologize. Then, when I apologize she begins to either play victim and talk about how much she has been hurt or she attacks me and complains about things I've done throughout my life that she didn't like.

I told my uncle that if my mom wanted us to speak, she would have to reach out to me because I was sick of always being the one to make amends and I did not want to put myself through another situation where I made myself vulnerable only to get berated and have my feelings, emotions and words minimized. My uncle understood because his mom-my grandma-is an extreme version of my mom.

After I told my uncle that I was open to speaking with my mom if she reached out, I got a video call from her but it wasn't her calling to talk about what happened. She called me while she was visiting my dad. I spoke with my dad while my mom held the phone. My mom chimed in later and asked how I was and she acted like nothing happened. I did not like that but I didn't want to discuss our issues while dealing with the emotions that came with looking at my sick dad.

Was this healthy? Probably not. Did I feel like I had a choice? No. My dad was no longer able to even pick up a phone and call me. He never answered his phone when I called and he eventually lost his phone. My mom was the only outlet I had to him and I didn't want to ruin that nor did I want to ruin those pleasant moments I had with my mom.

• • •

Video chatting can only substitute in-person contact to a degree. On the phone, my dad was rarely able to have an actual conversation. He was still able to say hi and ask how I was but beyond that, the conversation became difficult to hold. He had no memory so speaking about anything that had happened was out of the question. I told him stories about my life but I don't think they stuck in any way. There are moments with Alzheimer's where you say or do something and you know that your loved one is able to internalize that moment even if they can't express it. My experience has been that these moments are a lot more frequent in person.

Often when my dad talked, he would say things that made no sense or he would pronounce words wrong. The more syllables in a word, the more difficult it became for him to say. My mom tried to get my dad to talk for video messages that she sent me and other relatives. She sent videos of my dad repeating words after her. Even this was difficult for him because in the moment between hearing and speaking, he would forget a word or he would forget the last sound of a multi-syllable word and replace it with whatever was the next sound that came to his mind.

He was still visibly happy when we video chatted. He asked when I would visit. At times he knew who I was and other times he thought I was one of his cousins or brothers. When he didn't know how to respond to something, he sang or made random noises to try to make others laugh. Being a jokester was his way of bridging the gap of communication. Making people laugh does not always rely on the gift of remembering the past and he tried to use comedy as his way of communicating and having a good time with us. During this time, he had a new found love for dancing and enjoyed singing. Even though he had Alzheimer's, he was still evolving in his interests just like anyone else does as they get older.

With Alzheimer's, people may be in the same stage for months or years. When they are in a certain stage, you know they will eventually have a sharp decline but you may also be in denial. For instance, I knew that my father would eventually forget my name and my face but because it happened slower than I originally thought, I started to convince myself that it wouldn't happen.

When I wrote this chapter, I knew my dad would eventually lose his ability to speak and eat on his own. I knew he would cease to communicate 99% of the time. I knew he would eventually pass away. Yet, I convinced myself that for the rest of his life my dad was going to be making up words, joking, dancing and showing excitement whenever he saw me. It was hard for logic to win out.

There are two reasons I can think of for this. First, I simply didn't want it to happen; I was in denial. Second, what's the point of thinking about a future that will be even more heartbreaking? Why not just enjoy these moments?

I was sad that I was not physically closer to my dad. I felt like a bad son. As easily as I moved to Georgia I could have moved back to Minnesota. If I had a kid, wouldn't I want them next to me if I was in my dad's shoes? If I was a dad, wouldn't I want my kid to not have to worry about me and to follow their heart, their dreams, their desires?

Shiraz is a little too big to fly with me on an airplane. He would have to be checked in as cargo and that is something I would never do. The drive to Minneapolis is over 1,000 miles (1,609 kilometers). Yet, it is my dad. He is worth it. In five years will I regret not making this drive more often? Am I selfish for not wanting to live through

Minnesota winters and be around everything that will remind me of why I decided to move? I think so. These are my emotions. These are my thoughts. Life is not black or white. There is so much that goes into decisions that people make. I have learned not to judge why people may make a decision that makes no sense to me; I can't even make a decision and feel good about it. My own decisions don't always make sense to me.

12
More Grieving

When my dad was first diagnosed with Alzheimer's, I wish I would have taken advantage of the long-term memory he still had. I wish I would have picked his brain and asked him to tell me more stories about his past. I wish I would have milked every last bit of advice that I could from him. Instead, I was sad. I was angry. I was ignorant of what was to come.

From the very beginning my dad knew something wasn't right. I am grateful that he wasn't in denial. If we asked him a question, he would often tell us that he didn't remember. As he got worse, he would mention that he felt dizzy, confused and anxious. My dad was very self-aware, which I believe is a great trait to have, but that self-awareness seemed like it could have been torturous.

My dad used to say, "I don't know who I am anymore." I am sure that at some point most Alzheimer's patients are aware that something is not right. I believe that even when they can't communicate properly, they may still know something is wrong. Imagine waking up, not knowing where you are and knowing that you lack the memory to remember where you are. My dad may have lost his memory but he remembered that he could not remember.

• • •

I am terrified of Alzheimer's. It is a disease that I believe doesn't get talked about enough. We've all heard the word "Alzheimer's" and know that it means memory loss but many people don't know the pain it brings to families and to the patient. Many people don't know how to imagine what it would be like to have Alzheimer's. That is fair. If you haven't experienced it, how would you know? That's one reason I decided to write this book. I want people to know how Alzheimer's affects the patient and those around them.

When I started writing this book, I did not think about secrets that would have to be kept from my dad. I already explained how we had to pretend that his parents were alive. Well, since I began writing this book my dad's cousin's daughter died, my mom's parents passed away, my dad's oldest and closest brother died, two of his sisters died and one of his closest friends also passed away. We all knew that it wasn't a good idea to tell my dad about any of these deaths. He was already dealing with anxiety that was induced by his Alzheimer's and we did not want to trigger strong emotions from him that would make him angry or sad.

One reason is that while Alzheimer's patients may not remember things for long, the way something or someone made them feel may last for hours. In other words, their mind may forget but their body remembers.

They will sit in pain and not even remember what is agonizing them.

Why put him through the agony of grief when he won't remember? My response to that question is that a person deserves to know these things. He was very close to my grandpa. He loved his cousin's child, his siblings and friend. However, when you experience the disease long enough, you have to begin questioning the moralities behind being honest.

If we told my dad that his brother died, he would have been devastated, which is normal. Imagine though, that you are trying to come to grips with someone dying only to forget who you're grieving while you're crying. You know somebody died but you forget who. So you ask, "Did somebody die?" Once you are reminded of who died, you go back to step one and it's like learning about their death all over again.

Dealing with the death of others piles onto the grieving that is already being done by caretakers and loved ones of the person with Alzheimer's. One thing I did not think about until these situations began to arise is that people who are dealing with terminally ill loved ones still have other stressors in their lives. Almost six months after my cousin's passing, my grandpa died.

You know the question, "If you could have a meal with anyone dead or alive who would it be?" My answer was always my grandpa. The last time I saw him in person was 13.5 years before he died. Politics made it difficult to see my grandfather as an adult. I appreciated his wisdom and the life he lived. I wanted to learn from him. I don't remember where but once I heard someone say something akin to, "Parents are learning as they go. It is when they become grandparents that they are truly able to pass on their wisdom to their grandkids." His passing was unexpected. The day that I originally wrote this page marked seven days since his passing and I was still in denial of his death. I had not begun to process it yet.

I was grieving the two most important men in my life. All the while, life goes on. Work still calls. What is this society we have built? Most people are not allotted the time necessary to truly and fully grieve. My job at the time gave me five days of bereavement leave. I believe that's laughable. It's been seven days and I still am in denial of my grandpa's passing. Working and the thought of having to go to work blocks the energy that should be redirected toward grieving.

• • •

For the third time since moving to Georgia (and a few weeks after my grandpa passed away), I decided to take a trip north to visit my parents. I felt bad that my mom was alone and it was hard to grieve while being away from loved ones. I also went back because my sister was pregnant and I wanted to be there when her baby entered this world. I made almost daily trips to visit my dad when I went back and each time was more difficult than the last. Going to the nursing home and seeing his catheter full, his room not clean and him stressed out was infuriating. The nurses even lied about taking his vitals.

This all led to me having a conversation with my sister (a nurse) and her husband (a doctor). I state their professions because they were often able to provide insight that I didn't have. They mentioned how unless you have tons of money, this is as good as it gets. I laughed and said, "Yeah, right. You're telling me other facilities are run down and cockroach infested?" They responded with an affirmative answer. I bought it at the moment but while I am writing this, I don't know how much I believe it. They toured so many places before settling on the one my dad was at so they had to be telling the truth, right? America's healthcare system is a joke so it had to be true, right? I don't know.

I spoke to a social worker and she gave me a list of locations we could take my dad in Minnesota. Since my mom and I had also discussed having them move to Georgia, the social worker explained how multiple moves in a short period of time may do more harm than good as it could just lead to more confusion for my dad. I agreed. What also sucked was that you can't just transfer Medicaid to a new state. It all depends on the county and many counties throughout the country require the person to live in the state for at least 30 days before they receive any type of benefits.

• • •

During this trip, it was difficult to even take my dad for a short walk outside because it was late fall and it is cold in Minneapolis from November through March and sometimes April. I wanted to take him out to eat but I worried about him not being able to control his bowels. One day, I was having him change his clothes so we could go to a restaurant and I noticed that his pants were not clean. I changed him, which is something I never thought I'd do. He was oblivious to what he had done. I figured the chance of it happening again—no matter how small—was more than I was willing to risk just to go out to eat. Instead, we would go on walks inside the building.

We walked around his floor then took the elevator down to the first floor where we walked some more. We kept going up and down. Up and down. Our outdoor walks in the neighborhood had turned to indoor walks in a nursing home. The foundation was still there-the building was just different. These walks helped ease my dad's anxiety and made him forget about the annoyance of his catheter. His catheter is connected to his belly button and he is constantly complaining about pain. Every doctor who had looked at it said he was fine. Imagine having a tube sticking out of your stomach and not possessing the memory to comprehend what it is or why it's there.

Often after these walks, my dad would be tired. He would mention that he wanted to lay down and I would take him back to his room and he would lay in his bed. One time after I got him in bed, he told me how proud he was of me—something I'm glad he told me when he wasn't sick too. It felt good to hear it again. The next few minutes would usually consist of me explaining to him that I would be right back.

In order to leave, I had to lie. I would tell him that I was going to take a nap in the next room or going to take Shiraz for a walk or that I had to go to the bathroom. He'd always respond with, "Okay. You'll be back though, right?" I had no choice but to concur. Lying was the only way to leave. I hated doing it every time and every time I made sure he was actually tired and going to go to sleep. Sometimes I just stood in the room and looked out the window until he did fall asleep before leaving. It had become a lot easier to leave without him worrying than it

used to be. This was both a relief and saddening.

13
A Bright Spot?

My dad's ability to speak English eventually began to diminish. He could still say the basics and could sometimes comprehend what someone was saying but overall, a language he knew and was immersed in for over 40 years had started to evade him. His ability to speak and understand Farsi, his native tongue, was better but also diminishing.

While I was visiting, my sister had her baby. I would tell my dad in Farsi, "Pedar bozorg shodi," which translates to "You are a grandfather." He would respond with something like, "Dedan fozorg dodam?" He would try to repeat what I said but he couldn't do it which led to him inadvertently making up words in the process. I would continue to explain to him that his daughter had a baby.

Most of the time, he was not able to comprehend having a grandchild. He was able to understand that he had a daughter but trying to understand his connection to his daughter's daughter was too much.

On the rare occasions when he realized he had a grandchild, he would get excited. He would say, "All right! Yes! Let's go!" but this was short lived and he would quickly forget why he was excited. One time as we were going down the elevator to take a walk on the first floor, he looked at me and asked if my sister just had a baby. It was one of those fleeting moments of memory.

I do not understand how he could forget something within a second or fail to comprehend something and then have a random recollection and understanding of that very thing hours or days later. There were times when he suddenly transformed to his pre-Alzheimer's self. For 30-60 seconds, he would be completely coherent and knowledgeable of everyone around him. It was as if he was cured for those short periods of time. Those moments felt surreal. It was as if a switch was triggered in his mind. Were his memories still stored somewhere in his brain? Those short-lived moments of him seemingly snapping out of the disease convinced me that they were.

I also believe that there is a level of new memory being built even as the disease progresses into the mid to later stages. For example, moving a person with Alzheimer's comes with an adjustment period. They need to adjust to the new people and surroundings. Moving a person with Alzheimer's—even in the later stages—can be very stressful for them. To me, this means that some sort of memory is created that would require that adjustment to take place.

Another example of memory still being stored somewhere in my dad's brain was the emotions that were attached with the music he heard. While I was back in Minnesota, my dad's two cousins and I went to see my dad together. We hung out and they were trying to jog my dad's memory with stories from their past. My dad was very close with his cousins so they knew stories from my dad's childhood that neither me nor my mom knew.

One story was about when they drove my dad's car through the mountains of northern Iran. During the trip, my dad played music by an artist named Golpa. My cousin told me that my dad had a beautiful voice and that one song in particular used to make my dad so emotional that he would tear up. They then played that song and my dad sang along. He didn't remember all the words but he kept singing and singing. After a few minutes, his eyes got red and teary. An emotion was triggered. A memory had surfaced. One of my dad's cousins began to cry too. It was beautiful. It was confusing. It was something I am incredibly grateful that I got to experience. It was like getting a glimpse into who my dad was 20 years before I was born.

While these memories resurfaced others were still forgotten. During the same visit, my dad forgot he had kids. We had to be very specific with our questions. We had to ask, "Who is Omid?" or "Who is Shawdi?" and he would respond by saying that we are his kids or "They are one of us." At the same time, I could look at him and say I was his son and he wouldn't believe me. Yet, whenever I went to visit him he got excited as soon as he saw me. He couldn't always tell me who I was or how I was related to him but he could recognize something familiar about me from a distance every time I went to visit him.

Around this time he started to forget the names of his sisters too. He had three brothers and eight sisters. He could still list the names of the brothers but needed some help naming the sisters. Sometimes if we asked him what his kids' names are, he would begin to list the names of his siblings. Despite this huge loss of memory, or rather, because of it, he seemed to be happier.

His happiness seemed to stem from a level of ignorance. He was ignorant of the world he spent most of his life in. The life of bills, work and responsibilities were no longer weighing on him. This is not to say that he didn't still get worried or anxious.

There were times when my mom would receive 20 or more missed calls within a 10 minute span from my dad. Sometimes these calls would be accompanied by him anxiously begging to be picked up and taken home. Sometimes he would call and say nothing. He wouldn't respond to us yelling his name over the phone and after a minute, he would just hang up.

My dad working a phone was interesting. We would all get calls from him at random times but most of the time he didn't say anything. He'd call and you could faintly hear him conversing with others in his unit. You'd hang up and a few minutes (sometimes seconds) later, he'd call again and not say anything. You could scream his name into the phone and it was like he didn't even notice. Even if you pocket dial someone—which is more difficult to do with today's smartphones—you would think they could hear you screaming their name. It is just another one of the many mysteries of the disease. I'm sure many of you have, or know someone who has, a similar story. It may not be related to phone usage but still something the loved one did while they were sick that just made no sense.

Over time, his ability to use a phone continued to decrease and he eventually lost his phone. My mom had to buy a new phone for him that they kept at the nurses' station. As time went on and he spent more time at the nursing home, he became less anxious and began to acclimate to the environment. Earlier I mentioned how Alzheimer's patients seem to have a sense of memory in that they do not do well with a change of environment. They may forget that where they are is where they've lived for decades but moving them out of that home or from a nursing home they've lived in for a year can make them even more confused and anxious.

To me, this seemed to be the memory or the intelligence of the body rather than the mental self we so commonly identify with. It's like when we sweat; our bodies do it automatically to keep us cool, regardless of what we are thinking. To me, the intelligence of the body is like a plant in a pot. When you move a plant to a new pot, it takes some time for it to acclimate to its new home.

• • •

Sometimes when I went to visit my dad, he would be sitting in a sunroom located in the back of the floor he was on. When he would see me from afar, he would get up, smile and ask where I had been. He didn't know it was me but he knew that he knew me. He would politely say "goodbye" to all the people who were sitting near him before leaving with me. His goodbyes were in Farsi. He'd shake people's hands and say, "It was so good to see you." One time while he was doing his rounds, he went to a woman who was sitting down, shook her hand and caringly said, "I know you aren't feeling well but you will feel better. I hope to see you again soon." Nobody ever said anything back to him and it didn't seem like they noticed that he was speaking Farsi.

I did notice that whenever I went to visit him, the people he was around would smile. It was evident that they got happy for each other when someone visited. They may have had no idea what was going on but they still had the basic emotions and empathy that they always possessed. This was another example of the mind being gone but the soul staying the same. If anything, I'd say the true nature of my dad's soul sometimes seemed to shine brighter as the disease progressed. This is not to say that it was any easier to do previously simple things, like take him to a restaurant.

One chilly but sunny fall day in Minneapolis, my dad's cousin took us out to eat at one of the only Persian restaurants in Minnesota. I was nervous but hopeful that it would go okay with the two of us there to assist my dad. We made sure to sit in a corner that had a portable heater facing directly where my dad sat because he was always cold.

My dad was having a great time but did not seem to care about what anyone thought. He was loudly telling profane stories. He would tell stories that didn't make sense and then laugh. Sometimes what he said was no more than gibberish. He put parts of words together and sprinkled in made up words in his stories. Whenever he couldn't find a word or didn't know how to respond to someone he would say, "beluee beluee beluee!" This was fine and gave us all a good laugh when he did it. It never felt like the laughs were at him. It always felt like it was all of us laughing together. He was in a good mood when he made what sounded like no more than baby babble. The only problem was he didn't know when it was appropriate to "beluee beluee" and when it wasn't.

The babbling and nonsensical talk was not limited to this one instance at the restaurant. It had become incredibly common. He would do it at random times in any setting you could think of. He would often have full conversations by just saying "beluee beluee beluee." He would maintain the pitch and tone of a regular conversation but just replace every word with "belue." For example, imagine someone saying "Hi! How are you? What have you been up to?" like this: "Belue! Belue belue belue? Belue belue belue belue belue belue?" Unfortunately, we couldn't translate his babble and it was often just mimicking the tones and inclinations we made. I don't believe there was any meaning behind what he said. He was literally saying gibberish and just having a good time.

Many people at the restaurant knew my dad because we are Persian and many people from the small Persian community in Minnesota dined there. While we were sitting down at the restaurant, old friends came by to say hi to my dad and his cousin. When people came to say hi, my dad would give elaborate greetings. He'd say, "Heyyyy! How are you?" Then he'd make funny faces and tilt his head and body like a child when you tell them to make a funny face for a picture. He'd do this and then start telling a long story that made no sense and follow that by saying "Beluee beluee beluee beluee."

For example, someone asked how he was doing and my dad started pulling together pieces of a private conversation we just had and then built an elaborate story from that. I would have to interrupt and cut him short because he would turn a quick and polite greeting into an endless story. When they finally said goodbye, my dad would look at us and ask who he was just conversing with. He was very good at pretending like he knew who people were. He knew he didn't know a lot of things anymore. He knew he was dependent on his loved ones. It is interesting how he could forget so much but oftentimes remember that he couldn't remember.

In addition to being social and engaging in communication with others, my dad was starting to dance more than ever before. Before he was sick, he used to sometimes dance at parties but now if you played music and asked him to dance, he would get up and try to get everyone involved. The unit my dad stayed in would periodically bring someone in whose job was to help the residents with relaxation exercises. During one of these visits, my dad turned the relaxation exercises into a dance session. He started to dance with the instructor and tried to get other residents up and dancing. He got people clapping and smiling. While he may have ambushed the instructor's goal of a quiet relaxation session, my dad managed to lighten the mood and make the instructor and the residents laugh, smile and clap. His positive mood was infectious.

Unfortunately, this mood was not sustained throughout the day. There were still times throughout the day when he would become anxious and worry about where he was. Still, those instances were relatively mild in relation to previous episodes and they were easier to redirect. Oftentimes when he was left alone with no one to interact with, he would become more agitated and anxious. I know this because when I would go and visit and he was in the common area conversing with other residents, he seemed happy but when he would be in his room alone, he was more on edge and worried.

It was great to see my dad on the days he was in an elevated mood. Yet, there was still a sadness to being there. It was emotionally exhausting to see my dad in the state he was in; to have him not recognize me as his son; to be confined to only being able to see him indoors because it was too cold to go for a walk outside. It was sad to see the other residents and what Alzheimer's does to others, not just my dad.

Some of the residents had pictures of their younger selves on the walls outside their rooms. It gave me a glimpse into who these people were when they were younger. To contrast that with the walking zombies they appeared to be when I visited was heartbreaking. It felt cruel. These people all had lives that were stripped from them by this horrible disease. There was an opera singer who stayed on the same floor as my dad. Every time I visited I would hear her belting out a tune. She had a beautiful voice and used to perform in theaters. It was beautiful that while she had forgotten so much, a part of her still had this love for singing. At the same time, it is tragic how one day you can be on stage and fulfilling your dreams and the next day you are in a nursing home not knowing who your kids are.

This is all a reminder to enjoy the moment. A reminder to not take life too seriously. You truly never know what may happen. Many of us have said these words. Many of us believe them but so few of us live by them. This entire experience has given me constant reminders to just step back and not care so much about things that bring stress.

My dad went from stressing about money one day to not being able to work the next to eventually not remembering who I am. Alzheimer's puts everything into perspective. It allows you to see how quickly everything can be taken from someone. It allows you to see how a lifetime of problems can just disappear for someone simply because they lose their memory. The irony is that all those stressors may[5] have contributed to them developing the

---

[5] Milligan Armstrong, Ayeisha et al. "Chronic stress and Alzheimer's disease: the interplay between the hypothalamic-pituitary-adrenal axis, genetics and microglia." *Biological reviews of the Cambridge Philosophical Society* vol. 96,5 (2021): 2209-2228. doi:10.1111/brv.12750

disease but the disease made all of their previous problems irrelevant.

Having previous stressors become irrelevant does not minimize the severity of the disease in any way. A person with Alzheimer's loses the ability to recognize loved ones, create new memories, go to the bathroom, talk, know where they are and so much more. I think it's important for us to learn from tragedy and what I have learned is that very few of the things my dad stressed about really ended up mattering. Just enjoy life. Admittedly, "Just enjoy life" is easier said than done but I believe it is important to find resources to help us do just that. Whether it's therapy, self-help books, hanging out with friends or just being selfish and taking time for ourselves, we need to make sure we have the tools to be able to keep things in perspective. We only get one life. We never know when we will leave it.

I wish I realized all of this sooner and just appreciated the time I had with my dad even as the disease progressed. As I mentioned earlier, they may get on your nerves but take advantage of the time you have with them because they will only get worse and there will be things you'll never be able to do with them again. I'll never play basketball with my dad again. We will never play a game of backgammon or go on a vacation together again. We will never talk politics or watch sports together again. I will never sit across the dining room table and have a normal meal with him again. I will never see him cuddle in his bed with Shiraz again.

These were all things that I was able to do with him at some point while he had Alzheimer's but each of these were slowly stripped away. You just wake up one day and realize you will never be able to do something you did the day before. Again though, he did get on my nerves a lot.

He got on my nerves when he would ask the same questions over and over. He got on my nerves when he would move my stuff and I couldn't find them. He got on my nerves when he broke the bathroom lock and when he wore my shoes thinking they were his. I realize now that my frustrations were unnecessary. One, in the grand scheme of life, those problems were petty and it was pointless to get upset; it did nothing for anyone. Two, I should have just enjoyed those moments with my dad because he only got worse. If someone came over during the day he would constantly ask, "Was someone over earlier?" Eventually, you could walk out of a room for 10 seconds and come back in and he would think you just got there.

I mentioned earlier that I didn't know if I trusted my family's judgment on the nursing home they chose to place my dad. One day, I had a conversation with my sister and we discussed how much happier and safer my dad was since he left home. He no longer had to deal with my mom yelling at him and my mom no longer had to worry about him walking out of the house or leaving the stove on. My sister helped me realize that there were no good solutions but only "better" solutions. It took me a while to realize that no matter where he was, the worst was always to come.

• • •

Eventually, I went back to Georgia. I found myself wanting to pick up the phone and give my dad life updates. I was in the middle of buying a home again and I just wanted his advice. For a while, I didn't bother calling him because I knew he wouldn't answer. Then, I started to call every few days for a month and one day he answered and we video chatted for about 20 minutes. He kept asking me when I was coming home and where I was and a part of him seemed to be back. He was giving me advice. He was praising me and telling me to trust myself and that he trusts my judgment. After that call, I tried to call daily for a week but he never answered.

It just sucked not being able to see or talk to my dad. When I was back home, I was seeing him five to seven times each week. When I went back to Georgia, I could only see him through video chats when my mom went to visit him. While that was better than nothing, he eventually got to a point where he didn't understand anything that was said by the person on the other end of the call. My mom would have to repeat everything I said for him to understand it and even then, the chances of him understanding the most basic questions were slim.

By this point, April of 2022, he started to forget who I was more frequently. During our calls, my mom and I would tell him that I'm Omid, his son, and he did not seem to understand. He would just look at the screen, make a random noise, change the subject or say, "Oh, this is Omid? That's not Omid." There were times when he realized who I was. Those moments were fleeting, often less than a minute. When he did realize it, he was visibly emotional, like he missed me.

By September of 2022, the only person's name my dad remembered 100% of the time (or even more than half the time) was his own. After that, the people whose names he could remember most often were his parents' and then my mom's. Everyone else's name, including my sister and mine, were more difficult for him to remember. At this point, talking on the phone with him would derail me. Sometimes, I would hit a deep depression after talking to him. In those moments, it was hard to correlate that my emotions were tied to seeing my dad as a shell of himself but after a few days, I was able to make the connection.

My dad regretted not taking an extra trip to Iran before his father died and then later before his mother passed away. I knew I should have learned from his mistakes and regrets and visited him more often but the thought of making that drive was exhausting. I could have flown but I had nobody to watch Shiraz for more than a few days. Is a few days fair to my dad? It would have been better than nothing but was it the most I could do? Would I regret not making the 34 hour round-trip drive again? Was I just making excuses to make myself feel better? Is "an exhausting drive" really a valid reason?

These thoughts constantly ran in the background of my mind and added to the pain of having my father go through this disease. Was that pain self-induced? Did I deserve it? Was I being a victim when there was an easy solution? Maybe. If you know someone whose loved one has Alzheimer's, give them grace before judgment. Life is hard enough without this added layer.

Alzheimer's often affects the sick individual's children when they are adults. We take time to go see a parent who doesn't remember us and who is a shell of themselves. We then go home and carry that with us throughout our daily lives (children, work, bills, relationships). It is exhausting. Others drop everything for years to take care of a parent. They put relationships, friendships, vacations and their own needs on pause to take care of a parent. Some do more for a parent than that parent ever did for them.

14
Role Reversal

After a year and a half, I went back to visit my dad in Minnesota. While I was there, I usually went to see him around his lunch time. The lady who sat next to my dad at lunch every day was always happy when my dad had visitors. She would always talk to me with a smile. I always smiled back and politely nodded hello but I never understood a word she said.

She was like my dad's nursing home wife. Sometimes she thought my dad was her son and sometimes she thought my dad was her husband. Even though they didn't remember much, they both seemed to remember each other enough to sit next to each other regardless of where they were in the building. They might not have remembered anything but they were still able to create a bond and somehow remember that bond every day.

Often when I arrived during lunch time, my dad would be sleeping in a chair at his lunch table while his "wife" would mumble and smile at me. I would wake him up and he would often show zero emotion. He would just lift his head up and sit there. Sometimes it took up to twenty minutes to get him to notice me. When the food would arrive, he would continue to sit there. I would continuously say, "dad" and rub his shoulders until he became conscious of his surroundings again.

It was evident how healing touch was for my dad. Without touch, I am not sure if I would have been able to get him to notice me regardless of how much I tried to gain his attention with my voice. His "wife" always touched me when I was next to her. She would hold my hand or grab my arm. These people were starved for touch. They had no idea what was going on, where they were or who they used to be but they still required love and touch.

I wonder how Alzheimer's exacerbates depression. In the earlier stages, when one is still aware they are losing their memory, it is easy to see how depression can manifest. Imagine knowing that you will forget everything and everyone you know. In the later stages, it's harder to distinguish between depression and Alzheimer's. How much of my dad's zombie-like state was because of depression? Do depression and Alzheimer's grow together? I don't know but because of this zombie-like state my dad was no longer able to eat on his own.

It was a role reversal. Feeding a parent is weird. The person who used to feed me, protect me and pass wisdom on to me was now reliant on me. Even when I put his food on a utensil and raised it up to his mouth, he sometimes needed a reminder to open his mouth. After a few bites he would remember that he needed to open his mouth and take in the food when it was near his mouth. He was still able to chew and swallow although he took an exceptionally long time to chew, which isn't necessarily a bad thing.

Even though he enjoyed eating and we got to spend time together, it is not a memory I look back on fondly. The memory is filled with grief. I am grieving the loss of the part of him that knew how to feed himself. I'm sure one day I'll look back on those days and be grateful. Right now I am grieving the part of him that I lost more than I am thinking about the memories I created with the new person he had become.

What made it even harder was that one day while I was visiting my dad, I received a call from my mom. She told me the nursing home called her and told her that my dad had a seizure. This was strange to me because I had just arrived and my dad was sitting in his usual seat waiting for his food. My dad had never had a seizure in his life. We didn't know for two hours and now he was sitting without any supervision at a table. The staff apologized, he was checked by a doctor and he was ultimately okay. The whole thing was just an added layer to the stresses associated with the entire disease. In that moment, I was heated. I was angry that my dad was in that place and angry that he was sick. I was mad that he had a seizure and it was treated as no big deal but I was in a public place and I had to suppress my anger.

When you are around a young child, you get to experience things like their first time walking or their first word and these "firsts" can bring about immense joy and happiness that is acceptable to be expressed in public. When you are around someone with Alzheimer's, you experience their "lasts" or other heartbreaking moments in public and you sometimes swallow your emotions. You may have to learn to put on a mask in public during some of the most difficult moments of your life. Then you leave, arrive home and a few hours later the emotions may hit you and you have to be mindful of where they are coming from otherwise it can become a confused anger.

I often had to work up the energy to go visit my father. It was a 30 minute drive one way and when I arrived, my dad often looked helpless and zombie-like. Spending time with someone you love who was as sick as my dad is emotionally exhausting. Add a seizure on top of all that and you feel weighed down while having the energy sucked out of you. What made these trips even more exhausting was how difficult it was to leave. When I was ready to leave, I would tell him to stay seated and that I would be right back. I don't think he comprehended or remembered what I said because he would just follow me to the exit.

Oftentimes, I needed the help of a nurse to leave. I needed them to distract my father. This broke my heart. To have to turn my back on my dad and leave while he was being distracted felt wrong. I didn't have a choice but it still didn't feel right.

The other thing that made it hard to leave was seeing how much it helped him when I visited. It took a while to get him to come to reality but when he did, he seemed happy. When I would arrive, he would barely move his head or acknowledge me. After some time, he would walk with me and appear happy. We would go outside on the patio of the nursing home and he would pretend to wrestle with me like old times but he also had hallucinations.

I would play music that he liked and it didn't seem to interest him much anymore. Instead, it made him think we were at a party. He would point and start talking about people who were sitting across from us. Nobody was around us though. When we would walk through the door to go back inside, he would insist that the people he was hallucinating go before us. I'm thankful his hallucinations weren't negative or rooted in trauma.

One day when we were on the patio, my dad walked by a mini garden. He stared at the flowers. He enjoyed being around them. I mentioned earlier in this chapter that the memories of these visits were filled with grief. As I was writing this paragraph, I looked back on the note I had written in my phone about my dad looking at the flowers and when I saw it, it made me smile. I highly recommend writing down the memories you create because when you look back on your notes, some moments that you think were filled with only sadness might have had some joyful memories sprinkled in.

There were countless times when I wondered what quality of life my father had. I wondered if it was even worth it for him to be alive. By this point he was like a plant who forgot that he needed to aim for the sun. Yet, moments like us wrestling and him enjoying the fresh air and flowers outdoors were reminders that he was still capable of experiencing happiness and joy. Nothing made this more evident than when he hung out with his granddaughter.

One day, Shiraz, my sister, her husband and my one-and-a-half year old niece went to visit my dad. First, Shiraz, my sister and I went to get my dad so we could take him out on the patio where my niece and brother-in-law were waiting for him. The only person in this world whose lap Shiraz laid on was my dad's. Now, my dad didn't even seem to care about him. When I tried to direct his attention to Shiraz, he looked at him with disgust and told him to get away. Thankfully this was short lived and after a couple minutes he looked at Shiraz and smiled.

When we walked outside and my dad saw his granddaughter, he was full of joy. He recognized that she was a baby. He interacted with her the way most adults interact with young children. His tone, his happiness, his gentleness and his loving nature were all what you would expect from a grandfather. My dad was full of joy the entire time he was around her. Whenever he would turn around and see Shiraz or my niece, he would smile. Being around his granddaughter brought something out of my dad. He responded to simple questions like, "How are you?" and even danced a little bit for the first time in a long time. It was as if seeing his granddaughter brought my dad back to life… The dad we knew; the one who raised us.

My dad and the other patients showed similar reactions to my niece. They were all at various stages of the disease but regardless of the stage they were in, they knew they were seeing a young child. They were experiencing the pure joy that only a baby could bring. If some of them-like my dad-couldn't remember anything, how did they remember what a baby was? My dad needed help remembering how to sit down on a chair but he could recognize that a baby was a baby. He knew how to interact with her. He knew she needed to be protected. He was mindful of her when she was running around objects. Love and the admiration of babies seem to be as natural as breathing. When everything else is forgotten, we don't have to think about how to do these things. They are automatic.

If you saw my dad when we first arrived, it looked like there was no quality of life. However, no matter how much of a zombie he looked like and no matter how far removed he appeared to be from reality, there was always life waiting to be lived. Alzheimer's is nasty. At times, it makes you wish the person would pass so that they could be relieved from what appears to be a pointless life. Who are we, though, to decide that their life is pointless? Even though my dad couldn't name any of us, stand up on his own, go to the bathroom on his own or eat without assistance, he was still able to feel joy. That leaves me wondering if those moments of joy are worth all of the suffering.

When I saw the joy, I said yes; when I saw the zombie-like state he was in, I said no. Many people put their pets down out of love to end their pet's suffering even though their pet is still able to experience happiness and joy. How much does suffering need to outweigh joy to justify pulling the plug?

• • •

I was blessed to have a friend I was in close contact with during this visit to Minnesota. Looking back, I think I would have ended up in a dark place if it wasn't for this friend. Please, don't isolate yourself if your loved one has Alzheimer's and please check-in on your friends if their loved one has Alzheimer's. The grieving and caretaking can take a toll that we may not be fully aware of in that moment. I think part of this has to do with denial. The loved one is right there in front of you. Depending on what stage of the disease they're in, they may seem like their normal self. This can make it easy to deny that something is wrong.

I hated when people acted like my dad was okay. I hated when I would mention negative changes I saw in my dad and others would find a silver lining. I believe it is important to focus on the positives and what a person is still able to do throughout the disease but I do not believe that this should be done at the expense of negatives being swept under the rug. The negatives were things I wanted to talk about because they were painful for me to witness. I wanted my pain to be heard. Instead, I was often met with "yeah buts" or "at least he…" This was an isolating feeling. It made me feel like I was overreacting with my emotions. Instead of having people to talk out my feelings with, I had people who made me feel like my feelings weren't based in reality.

15
How Long Should I Wait?

Since I began writing this book, I have struggled with when to end it. Do I publish it while he's still alive and share it with him? Do I end the book right here? Do I wait until he passes away? It had been eight years since my dad sent me the article about Pat Summit and almost a year had passed since I wrote the previous chapter. During that time, I was laid off from my job, went through a year of unemployment and I hadn't spoken to or seen my dad.

The last time I was in Minnesota, my mom and I got into an argument. Since childhood, my mother punished me when she was mad at me by ignoring me. I remember my mom not talking to me for a month when I was eight years old because I did something wrong. Again, I was eight... This pattern of ignoring me never went away. In addition to being ignored, my childhood consisted of hearing my mom

often say things like:

"I hope I die so I don't have to deal with you all anymore."

"God, what did I do to deserve this family?"

"Shut up or I'll shut you up."

My mother treated my sister and I like we were

adults who should have known everything and never made

mistakes. If we upset our mom in the slightest, we were

punished but never told what we did wrong and we were

never told what we should have done instead. In fact, every

time my mother ignored me it was my responsibility to

approach her and apologize even if I felt like I did nothing

wrong.

My dad's parenting style was the opposite of my

mom's. He was gentle and would try to understand my

emotions. He would give me advice and when he was upset

with something I did, he would explain why. He also

wanted peace in the home and always made me apologize

to my mom because my mom would get mad at him for standing up for us. My mother and I being on bad terms was bad for their marriage. To this day, I don't feel like that was fair to me but I understand where he was coming from. Unfortunately, I believe it set a bad precedent that led, in part, to me not seeing him for a year.

During my last trip, my mom did something I explicitly asked her not to do. Since she has done things I have asked her not to many times in my life, I got upset. We got into an argument and the next morning I went to apologize. I told her that what she did upset me but I could have handled the conversation better. She ignored me. She has continued to ignore me. I am fed up with having to always be the bigger person. Not once in my life has my mom ever said, "I'm sorry," or "I was wrong." She has shared secrets I've begged her not to tell, she has made fun of me in front of my friends, her friends and my teachers and she has withheld love as punishment since I was a child.

This is just a summary of issues I've had with my mom and far from all encompassing. I hope our society starts realizing that it takes a lot for grown children to not speak to a parent. It happens after years-or decades-of abuse. My mom was very emotionally and verbally abusive towards me throughout my life and I did my best to tiptoe around our issues while writing this book but I cannot do that anymore. My poor relationship with my mom meant I no longer had a place to stay in Minnesota which led to me not being able to see my dad for 14 months.

16
When in Rome

Shortly after I had last seen my dad, I met a woman from Italy and we eventually got engaged. She came to visit me a couple times in the United States and now it was time for me to go visit her in Rome (I was employed again). This trip was to coincide with me visiting my cousins in Italy and their mom, my aunt, who was visiting from Iran. I had not seen my aunt or cousins in over 15 years.

There was only one problem: I had nobody to watch my dog, Shiraz. I wanted him to be with someone familiar who I knew I could trust beyond all doubts. So, I did what I did many times before; I packed up my car and on Saturday, September 14, 2024, I drove north to Minnesota so that one of my trusted friends could take care of Shiraz while I was gone. We arrived the next day.

I had two full days between my arrival in Minnesota and my departure to Rome. The day before I left, I went to go see my dad. I did not know what to expect. I was prepared for the worst. At least, I was prepared for what my mind thought could be the worst. When I walked into my dad's room, he looked like a zombie. I started to cry. I tried to stop the tears but I couldn't. He looked worse than I could have imagined.

When I entered his room, he was talking to himself (or having a conversation with someone who was not there) but nothing he said was intelligible. Eventually, he stopped talking and just stared at me like he was studying me. It was as if he recognized me and he was trying to figure out who I was. This was short-lived and he soon went back to the conversation he was having. I wonder how the brain processes speech for people who are at this stage of dementia. Were the sounds that were coming out of my dad's mouth intelligible to his brain?

The sounds he was making sounded like he was attempting to speak Farsi. This means that his brain still remembered sounds that were learned. For example, babies aren't born saying the guttural sound "kh" but it is a common sound in Farsi that native speakers learn during childhood and my dad was still using that sound in his speech. Even if it was in the most basic way, it seemed like his brain was still able to remember something.

Soon after I arrived, a nurse came in to take him to dinner. This was the first time I visited my dad when he was unable to get up or walk on his own. He had to be lifted into a wheelchair and wheeled to the dining area. The person who taught me how to shoot a basketball, the most efficient way to run and how to throw a football could no longer stand up on his own. Honestly, I don't remember anything from this visit beyond that moment. This is the last memory I have of my dad.

• • •

The next day, I went to Rome. I was not in a good mood while I was there. I have traveled a lot and always loved exploring new cities but this trip did not have the joy of travel that I was used to. I had no energy and, at the time, I did not know why. On the day I was supposed to travel from Rome to Milan to see my family, I cancelled. I did not have the energy to make that trip.

I think I have always downplayed how heavy grief is. Grief doesn't hit all at once. It is a constant emotional drain. It can be hard to recognize the effect grief has on our emotions and energy. I saw my dad on a Tuesday. I got on a plane the next day and went to Amsterdam for a connecting flight before arriving in Rome on Thursday. I explored Rome on Friday and when Saturday came around and it was time to get on the train to visit my family, I did not have it in me.

No matter how much I tried to convince myself to go, I could not muster up the energy to make the trip. This moment, along with many moments before and after, made me worried about my health. I felt like I was aging really fast and it scared me. I now realize that it has been grief. Even though I now know what it is, it is still difficult to accept. The moments that lead to feelings triggered by grief can feel so distant from the pain that causes them that it can be difficult to pinpoint why we feel the way we do.

People often say that journaling or writing can help us process our emotions. There have been times where the only way I felt like I could get my emotions out while writing was to slam the keyboard and write something like, "A;HISFOFIHSDAAFSHIOVBR3UW9[E."

I don't think anything heals us from grief. It is something we have to experience. We can do things to momentarily feel better and take our minds off the grief but when we have those moments of silence, the grief creeps right back in.

I never made it to Milan to see my family. A week after I arrived in Rome, I landed back in Minnesota. Two days later, Shiraz and I were back on the road to Georgia.

While Italians can visit the United States without a visa, my fiance needed a visa so she could come to the U.S. for us to get married and subsequently apply for a Green Card. Five-and-a-half months had passed since we applied for her visa. I left Minnesota on September 28, 2024, not knowing when I would see my dad or fiance again. I ended up seeing them both in December.

17

Loss and Gain

In the beginning of December, my wife had her visa

interview in Italy. Her visa was approved and she was set to

arrive in the United States on December 20th. On December

15th, my dad's cousin called me and told me that my dad

was in bad shape. The next day, I called his memory care

unit and spoke with a nurse. She told me that I should go

home and say my goodbyes. Two days later, on December

18th, my mom sent me a picture of her, my dad's cousin,

his wife and their son next to my dad who was lying in his

bed. My dad looked terrible. I didn't think he could look

worse than when I had visited him in September but he did.

He looked like a severed tree branch whose leaves were

still green but slowly turning brown. You could tell his

body was ready to return to the earth.

At this point, it had been one-and-a-half years since I had last spoken with my mom. She called me and asked if I wanted to video chat with my dad. I said no. In that moment, after seeing the picture that I had just seen, I didn't even know what to say. Right now, I know exactly what I would have said but in that moment, I could not gather a single thought.

I was planning my trip back to Minnesota to see my dad but my fiance was scheduled to arrive late on the night of December 20th. I could not leave Georgia right away because I had to wait for her to arrive first. Approximately 12 hours after my mom sent that picture of my family around my dad, he died in the middle of the night on Thursday, December 19th.

I wasn't there. My sister wasn't there. His brothers and sisters lived in Iran and could not be there with him. When he passed, he passed alone. No family within the city he passed away in when he died. He deserved better. Did I prioritize myself too much? In the grand scheme of things, would it have made a difference if I was by his side when he passed or if I spent more time with him instead of moving away? Maybe he would have had a few seconds of lucidity and we would have shared one last memory the night he died. Maybe he would have passed away more peacefully. Maybe our bond and my love could have helped prolong his life if I never moved.

• • •

My fiance's flight was delayed and she arrived in Atlanta in the middle of night on Saturday, December 21st. Four hours later, we were on the road to Minnesota. We arrived on Sunday after an overnight stop in Missouri and on Monday we went to go see my dad's body for the final time. When we arrived at the cremation center that was holding his body, we were joined by my mother, my cousin (dad's nephew), two of my dad's cousins and one of my dad's friends.

After the staff went over some paperwork with my mother and I, we all proceeded to go into the room where they placed my dad's body for us to say our final goodbyes. When we opened the door, he was immediately visible and I saw him laying on a steel cart next to the back wall of the room. I walked over to him and he looked like he was smiling. I could not believe he was dead. I kept expecting him to jump up and try to scare me as a joke. This wasn't a fleeting feeling. Every time I was next to his body, I kept expecting him to lunge at me with a laugh.

After walking over to him and feeling how ice cold his body was, I sat down. I wanted everyone else in the room to say what they wanted to say and experience what they wanted to experience before I had a moment alone with my dad for the final time. Eventually, everyone but my soon-to-be wife and I were in the room with my dad's body. This was her first time ever seeing my dad. What an introduction.

The first thing I did was call a couple of my aunts and cousins overseas so they could see my father for the last time and say their final goodbyes. Then, it was my turn. I touched the head block that my dad's head was resting on and it was solid. No living person could have tolerated laying their head on something so hard for so long. This served as another reminder that he was dead. The entire time I was hoping it was all a joke. I held on to this unrealistic hope that he was alive but the head block and his ice cold skin were reminders that he was gone and never coming back.

I apologized to my dad. I apologized for not being around more when he was sick and before he died. I told him I loved him and thanked him for everything he had done for me and everything he had given me. I told him he was a great dad. I introduced him to my soon-to-be wife. I pleaded with him to come back.

• • •

Sometimes the most random things at the most random moments will remind me of my dad. One time I looked up at a cloud and it reminded me of all the times my dad used to tell me what he thought random clouds looked like. Other examples are an insurance commercial reminding me of how I used to be on my parents' insurance when I was younger or I could be eating hummus and remember how my dad used to eat tahini in the mornings. The thing that broke me the most was a cat meme about a cat reminiscing about his deceased dad. I sobbed uncontrollably watching a cat meme video.

Grief is so complex. It doesn't go away. The pain may not be constant but when it arises, it is as painful as the first time. I have learned that the more time passes, the more I grieve the present and the future. I went on vacation and grieved that my dad couldn't join me and that I couldn't tell him about it. I grieved not being able to enjoy the Minnesota Timberwolves make deep playoff runs with him. I grieve that I won't be able to see him develop a relationship with his granddaughter.

When I was saying goodbye to my niece after my dad's funeral, I started to cry. My tears were not because I was going to miss my niece but because my dad wasn't going to experience the joy of watching her grow up. I grieve because I lost him and I grieve his losses.

His death has made me believe in time travel. For my entire life, he was there. He was real. He existed. My brain cannot fathom that he no longer exists in a physical form. I feel like I should still be able to travel to wherever he is or once was and be able to reach out and touch him. He feels so close for someone who is no longer here.

Immediately after my dad died, I heard from family, friends and one of my dad's old friends even reached out to me. A couple of my friends really showed up and were very supportive of me between the time of my dad's death and his funeral. After my dad died, the only time anyone even brought up my dad was a cousin when we were catching up and one of my aunts who reached out to me on my dad's birthday. Aside from that, nobody ever checked in on me. Some of you might be thinking, "Poor Omid. People don't know they should reach out if you don't say anything." People know. Older relatives know. They have dealt with loss. Our culture is broken.

Grieving doesn't end after a funeral. Oftentimes, it is just ramping up. Maybe it's because of distance. Maybe it's because people don't know what to say. Maybe it's both. Maybe it's something else. If your friend has experienced loss, check in on them over time.

• • •

Writing this book made me feel close to my dad and allowed me to recognize, label and process all the feelings I had when I was around him while he was sick. My dad began to show signs of dementia after I graduated college so I never got to experience a true adult relationship with him. Writing this book allowed me to reflect on who I am today and how my dad helped shape my adult years through the stories he told me and the lessons he instilled in me during my formative years.

Growing up, I was anxious during interactions with adults. I was anxious when I was around strangers. I didn't even like being around my parents' friends. My dad taught me to snap out of this. When we went out, he made me pay (with his money) and interact with cashiers. He always told me to ask questions and that the worst thing that could happen is that someone will say "I don't know" or "no." He taught me to trust myself and to be confident. He taught me that there is nobody in this world who is above me and there is nobody in this world who is below me; to treat everyone with respect and to not fear anyone. He taught me to never punch down and to stand up for those who are bullied. It took a while but once I became an adult, those lessons started to mold me.

There are still plenty of times when I wish I could dig into my dad's wisdom and ask him for advice but I know that opportunity has passed. Just because we surpass 18 years old or move out of our parents home doesn't mean we don't need our parents anymore. If anything, as an adult, we need our parents' wisdom and advice just as much as we did when we were kids. This is why I hold a random blue piece of paper so close to my heart. My dad used to write me notes to encourage me to do better in school and life. He saw my potential years before I did. The next two pages contain the contents of that letter edited for clarity.

• • •

"Omid, please read this page carefully. As your dad, I would like to see you be successful. Caring fathers who love their kids want to see their kids be good to their family and to society. These are a few points I would like to make:

Please get rid of all the negativity. This means you can do anything that you desire but you have to be determined, focused, active and follow up on your tasks.

You can make a plan and follow your dream. For example, if you want to be a basketball player, you know you have to work hard. You have to get up early in the morning, go to the park and practice for 5 to 6 hours each day regardless of if it is raining, sunny or humid. In this case, you have to think big. You are trying to accomplish your goal. No matter what is going to happen, your brain-your real engine-make sure your engine is tuned and is not lazy. For example, if you say, 'I am tired because I slept 7 hours instead of 8,' your brain automatically shuts down but if you say, 'I am going to do it no matter what,' your brain will cooperate with you to reach your goal.

Omid, you have to be patient. This is the best time. You can change and learn from my mistakes. Unfortunately, you are making some of the same mistakes I made when I was your age. I am regretful but I did not have anybody to guide me. You are lucky that I am willing to put in my time to make sure you are on the right track. Just so you know, I am not just your dad. I am also your best friend."

Omid
Please read this Page Carefully

As Your Dad , I would like to see you successful, and as a
Caring father which he loves his kids the most wants to see their
kids to be good or to their family, and their society (not political)
These are few Points I would like to make

- Please get rid of all The negativity. This means You Can
Do anything that You Desire, but You have to be
Determind, Focus, active, follow up On Your Tasks

- You Can make a Plan & follow Your Dream. for example
if You want To be a Basketball Player You Know You
have to work hard. You have to get up early morning
go To The Park & Practice for 5 to 6 hrs a day regardless of
if it is rainny, suny, or humid. in This Case to you
think Big, You are Trying To accomplish your
goal. no matter what is going to happen (Your Brian is
You real engine, make sure your engine is Tune & is
not lazy. for example if You say I am tired, because
I sleep 7hrs instead &, your Brain automaticly our

shut down. but if You say I am going to do J. no matter what. Your Brain will Cooperate with You to reach to your goal.

Omid You have To be Patient. this is The Best Time You Can change & learn from my mistakes.

Unfortunatly You are making some of my mistakes when I was Your age & I am Regreted, but I Did not have anybody to gevide me, but You are luck I am willing to Put my Time to make sure You are in the Right Track

Just You know (I am not Just Your Dad. I am also Your Best Friend

Love may not be the cure for Alzheimer's but I believe it is

the closest thing there currently is.

My dad a year before his Alzheimer's diagnosis.

www.ingramcontent.com/pod-product-compliance
Lightning Source LLC
Chambersburg PA
CBHW060321050426
42449CB00011B/2585